TypeScript
Interview Questions and Answers

X.Y. Wang

Contents

3 Intermediate   67

5 Expert 165

6 Guru   **225**

Chapter 1

Introduction

Welcome to "TypeScript: Interview Questions and Answers". Whether you're preparing for a TypeScript job interview, or you're a seasoned developer looking to review and expand your TypeScript knowledge, this book is designed to be a comprehensive and valuable resource for you.

TypeScript is a powerful, open-source programming language developed and maintained by Microsoft. It's a statically typed superset of JavaScript that adds optional types, classes, and modules to the language, while also supporting tools for large-scale JavaScript applications.

The popularity of TypeScript has been growing steadily. It's not just being used for front-end development—TypeScript is also widely used on the server-side with Node.js.

Its ability to add robust type-checking to JavaScript, while maintaining compatibility with existing JavaScript code and libraries, has made it a favorite among developers and companies alike.

This book is organized into five levels: Basic, Intermediate, Advanced, Expert, and Guru. Each level addresses a different depth of knowledge and complexity, allowing you to progress through the book as your understanding of TypeScript deepens.

The "Basic" level covers fundamental aspects of TypeScript, such as data types, variables, interfaces, classes, and functions. This level is designed for beginners and those new to TypeScript.

The "Intermediate" level delves into more complex topics such as decorators, namespaces, type guards, and static properties. Here, we also start discussing TypeScript with Node.js and the concepts of index types and optional chaining.

The "Advanced" level takes a deep dive into TypeScript with front-end frameworks, union types, higher-order functions, mixin classes, and third-party type definitions. Topics such as abstract classes, type narrowing, and the strict mode in TypeScript are also covered.

The "Expert" level is designed for those who are comfortable with TypeScript and want to understand the intricacies of setting up and configuring a build process for a TypeScript project. It also discusses topics such as handling transpilation of TypeScript into different versions of ECMAScript, working with web workers, and strategies for migrating a large JavaScript codebase to TypeScript.

Finally, the "Guru" level is for those who want to delve into architectural patterns, enforcing architectural constraints using TypeScript's type system, performance optimization, and advanced error handling. This level also covers strategies for gradually adopting TypeScript in a large JavaScript project and using TypeScript effectively with data science or machine learning libraries.

By the end of this book, you should have a solid grasp of TypeScript, from its basic to advanced concepts. You'll be equipped with a wide range of knowledge that will help you ace your TypeScript interviews and use TypeScript more effectively in your projects.

So, let's embark on this journey together to unravel the intricacies of TypeScript, one question at a time. Enjoy the read!

Chapter 2

Basic

2.1 What is TypeScript and how is it different from JavaScript?

TypeScript is a superset of JavaScript that combines the flexibility and dynamism of JavaScript with the benefits of a type system, including static type checking, improved tooling, and better code organization. It is developed and maintained by Microsoft, and the language's syntax and features are designed to be compatible with modern JavaScript standards, including ECMAScript 2015 (ES6) and beyond.

The main difference between TypeScript and JavaScript is that TypeScript introduces static typing to help catch type-related errors during development, while JavaScript is a dynamically typed language. This enables better code analysis, refactoring support, and autocompletion while writing code. TypeScript also includes support for interfaces, abstract classes, and other advanced object-oriented features.

Here's a comparison between TypeScript and JavaScript code to demonstrate some differences:

JavaScript:

```
function greet(person) {
  return "Hello,␣" + person;
}

const user1 = "Jane␣User";
const user2 = [0, 2, 4];

console.log(greet(user1)); // Hello, Jane User
console.log(greet(user2)); // Hello, 0,2,4 (unexpected behavior)
```

TypeScript:

```
function greet(person: string): string {
  return "Hello,␣" + person;
}

const user1 = "Jane␣User";
const user2 = [0, 2, 4]; // TypeScript will show an error here

console.log(greet(user1));
console.log(greet(user2)); // TypeScript will show an error here,
    preventing unexpected behavior
```

In this example, the TypeScript code introduces a type annotation for the 'person' parameter in the 'greet' function, ensuring that only string values are accepted. This helps prevent unexpected behavior during runtime.

Here is a summarized comparison table between Type-Script and JavaScript features:

Feature	TypeScript	JavaScript	
Typing	Static (Optional)	Dynamic	
Type inference	Yes	Yes	
User—defined type guards	Yes	N/A	
Interfaces	Yes	N/A	
Enums	Yes	N/A	
Namespaces	Yes	N/A	
Abstract classes	Yes	N/A	
Optional chaining	Yes (ECMAScript optional with Babel)	Yes (ECMAScript 2020)	
Nullish coalescing	Yes (ECMAScript optional with Babel)	Yes (ECMAScript 2020)	

In summary, TypeScript is an extension of JavaScript that adds optional static typing to the language, enabling better tooling, code organization, and error prevention. Developers can leverage TypeScript's features to write more robust and maintainable codebases while still targeting standard JavaScript when compiling.

2.2 Can you list some benefits of using TypeScript?

TypeScript is a powerful, statically-typed superset of JavaScript that brings many benefits to JavaScript developers. Here are some of the most important benefits of using TypeScript:

1. **Type Safety**: TypeScript enforces type checking during the compile time, which helps identify and eliminate many issues before execution. It prevents type-related

errors and leads to more robust and maintainable code.

```
function sum(a: number, b: number) { return a + b; }
```

2. **Better Tooling and IDE Support**: Thanks to TypeScript's static typing, IDEs have improved tooling support, like autocompletion, navigation, and refactoring options that make the development process smoother and more interactive.

3. **Readability and Maintainability**: TypeScript encourages developers to be more explicit about their intent with the variable types, function signatures, and interfaces. It enhances code readability and makes maintaining large codebases easier.

```
interface Person { name: string; age: number; }
```

4. **Catch Errors Early**: Since TypeScript compiles to JavaScript and introduces static typing, it allows developers to catch errors and issues early and fix them at the development stage. This prevents many runtime bugs and reduces debugging time.

5. **Object-Oriented Programming Features**: TypeScript supports features from object-oriented programming, such as classes, interfaces, inheritance, and access modifiers, which are familiar to developers coming from

OOP languages like Java and C#. This can lead to more organized and structured code.

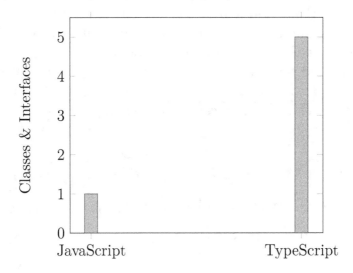

6. **Gradual Adoption**: TypeScript can be gradually adopted in any JavaScript project. You can start by adding type definitions to existing JavaScript files and then migrate the codebase in stages.

7. **Strong Ecosystem**: TypeScript is well-supported by a large community and has a rich ecosystem of third-party libraries with type definitions. It is tightly integrated with the JavaScript ecosystem and can be used with popular libraries like React, Angular, and Vue.

8. **Better Collaboration**: Type information in TypeScript code promotes better collaboration among devel-

opers, as it makes it easier for them to understand the code, reuse components, and contribute to the codebase.

To summarize, TypeScript offers numerous advantages to JavaScript developers, including type safety, improved tooling, better readability, maintainability, early error-catching, OOP features, gradual adoption, a strong ecosystem, and enhanced collaboration. Incorporating Type-Script into your development process can lead to more robust, efficient, and well-structured applications.

2.3   What are data types in Type-Script and can you provide examples of each?

In TypeScript, data types are used to specify the types of values that can be assigned to variables or used as function parameters and return values. TypeScript is a statically typed language, which means the types of values are determined at compile-time. This allows the TypeScript compiler to catch type-related errors early on and improves code readability.

Here is a list of basic data types provided by TypeScript:

1. Boolean

The Boolean data type represents a true or false value. For example:

```
let isActive: boolean = true;
let isInactive: boolean = false;
```

2. Number

The Number data type represents both integer and floating-point values. TypeScript uses the floating-point number format defined by the IEEE 754 standard. For example:

```
let integer: number = 10;
let floatingPoint: number = 3.14;
```

3. String

The String data type represents a series of Unicode characters. In TypeScript, you can use single or double quotes (or even backticks for template literals) to define string literals. For example:

```
let companyName: string = 'TypeScript Inc.';
let website: string = "https://www.typescriptlang.org/";
let welcomeMessage: string = `Hello, welcome to ${companyName
    }!`;
```

4. Array

Arrays are collections of elements of the same type. In TypeScript, you can define arrays in two ways, either by specifying the 'Array<Type>' syntax or using the 'Type[]' syntax. For example:

```
let numbers1: number[] = [1, 2, 3, 4, 5];
let numbers2: Array<number> = [6, 7, 8, 9, 10];
let names: string[] = ['Alice', 'Bob', 'Cathy'];
```

5. Tuple

Tuples in TypeScript allow you to represent a fixed-size array where each element can have a different type. For example:

```
let person: [string, number] = ['Alice', 30];
```

6. Enum

Enums provide a way of giving friendly names to sets of numeric values. For example:

```
enum Color {
  Red,
  Green,
  Blue,
}
let primaryColor: Color = Color.Red;
```

7. Any

The Any data type is useful when you don't know the type of value you are working with. It allows you to assign any type of value to a variable. For example:

```
let data: any = 'Hello';
data = 42;
data = [1, 2, 3];
```

8. Void

The Void data type is the absence of having any type at all. It is commonly used as the return type of functions that do not return a value. For example:

```
function printMessage(message: string): void {
  console.log(message);
}
```

9. Null and Undefined

Null and Undefined are subtypes of all other types in TypeScript. Their values can be assigned to any type of variable. For example:

```
let nothing: null = null;
let absence: undefined = undefined;
```

10. Never

The Never data type is used for values that never occur, for instance, in functions that always throw an error or have an infinite loop. For example:

```
function throwError(message: string): never {
  throw new Error(message);
}

function infiniteLoop(): never {
  while (true) {}
}
```

11. Object

The Object data type represents non-primitive types in TypeScript. It can be used to represent any object type value, except for primitive types (number, string, boolean, null, undefined, symbol). For example:

```
let person: object = { name: 'Alice', age: 30 };
let animals: object[] = [{ name: 'dog' }, { name: 'cat' }, {
    name: 'fish' }];
```

These are some of the basic data types in TypeScript that you may encounter while using the language. There are also advanced type features like union types, intersection

types, type aliases, and more which provide additional
flexibility and control over your TypeScript code.

2.4   How do you install TypeScript and compile a .ts file?

To install TypeScript and compile a .ts file, follow these
steps:

1. Install Node.js: TypeScript is a superset of JavaScript
and requires Node.js to work. Download and install Node.js
from the following link: [https://nodejs.org/en/download/]
(https://nodejs.org/en/download/)

2. Install TypeScript: After installing Node.js, open your
terminal or command prompt, and type the following
command to install TypeScript globally:

```
npm install -g typescript
```

3. Create a '.ts' file: Create a TypeScript file with the extension '.ts'. For example, create a file named 'example.ts'.
Add this code to the file:

```
function greet(name: string) {
    return 'Hello, ' + name + '!';
}

let user = 'TypeScript User';
console.log(greet(user));
```

4. Compile the TypeScript file: In your terminal or com-

mand prompt, navigate to the directory containing the 'example.ts' file. Run the following command to compile the TypeScript file to JavaScript:

```
tsc example.ts
```

This command will generate a new file named 'example.js' containing the JavaScript equivalent of your TypeScript code.

5. Execute the compiled file: Now that you have the compiled JavaScript file, you can execute it using Node.js:

```
node example.js
```

This command will return the output 'Hello, TypeScript User¡.

Here's a summary of the process:

Install Node.js: Download and install Node.js from `https://nodejs.org/en/download/`.

Install TypeScript: Run `npm install -g typescript` in the terminal/command prompt.

Create a .ts file: Create a file named `example.ts` with the sample TypeScript code.

Compile the TypeScript file: Navigate to the directory containing the `example.ts` file and run `tsc example.ts`.

Execute the compiled file: Run `node example.js` to see the output 'Hello, TypeScript User¡.

2.5 What are the different ways to declare variables in Type-Script?

In TypeScript, there are three main ways to declare variables: 'var', 'let', and 'const'. Each has its own set of characteristics and use-cases. Here is a detailed explanation of each one:

1. 'var': This is the traditional way to declare a variable in JavaScript. Variables declared using 'var' are function-scoped, meaning they are only accessible within the function they are defined in. However, if a variable is declared outside any function, it becomes a global variable. Additionally, 'var' declared variables are hoisted, meaning they are moved to the top of their scope and can be used before the actual declaration in the code.

```
function exampleVar() {
    if (true) {
        var x = 10; // x is function-scoped, not block-scoped
    }
    console.log(x); // This logs 10, because x is available in the
        entire function
}
```

2. 'let': Introduced in ECMAScript 2015, 'let' allows us to create block-scoped variables. With 'let', variables are

only accessible within the block they are declared. This is generally considered a more predictable and safer way to declare variables. 'let' declared variables are not hoisted.

```
function exampleLet() {
    if (true) {
        let y = 20; // y is block-scoped
    }
    console.log(y); // This throws a ReferenceError, because y is
        not accessible outside the block
}
```

3. 'const': This is also a block-scoped variable like 'let', but with an added restriction - you cannot change the value of a 'const' variable once it has been assigned. This makes 'const' the ideal choice for declaring constants or any variable that should not change its value during execution. 'const' declared variables are also not hoisted.

```
function exampleConst() {
    const z = 30; // z is block-scoped and has a constant value
    z = 40; // This throws a TypeError, because trying to change
        the value of a const variable is not allowed
}
```

In summary, you should generally use 'let' for block-scoped variables that will change their value, and 'const' for block-scoped variables with a constant value. Avoid using 'var' in TypeScript to prevent issues related to function scoping and variable hoisting.

Here is a table summarizing the differences:

	var	let	const
Scope	Function	Block	Block
Hoisting	Yes	No	No
Can be reassigned	Yes	Yes	No

2.6   Can you explain the concept of 'interfaces' in TypeScript?

In TypeScript, the concept of interfaces is used to define the structure of a specific object or a set of objects, ensuring that they strictly adhere to this structure. Interfaces are useful for defining contracts within a codebase and can be utilized alongside classes to enforce specific object shapes.

Essentially, an interface in TypeScript consists of a collection of key-value pairs, where keys are the property names and values are the types of their corresponding values. They provide a way of defining custom types without implementing the logic behind those types. This is mainly useful for type checking and code maintainability.

Here's a simple example of an interface:

```
interface Point {
  x: number;
  y: number;
}
```

In this example, we define a 'Point' interface representing a point in two-dimensional space. It has two properties, 'x' and 'y', which must be of the 'number' type.

Now, let's say we have a function 'computeDistance' that takes two 'Point' objects as arguments and calculates the distance between them:

```
function computeDistance(p1: Point, p2: Point): number {
```

```
    const dx = p1.x - p2.x;
    const dy = p1.y - p2.y;
    return Math.sqrt(dx * dx + dy * dy);
}
```

When we call this function with objects that adhere to the 'Point' interface, TypeScript will not show any errors:

```
const pointA: Point = { x: 0, y: 0 };
const pointB: Point = { x: 3, y: 4 };
console.log(computeDistance(pointA, pointB)); // 5
```

However, if we try to pass an object that does not strictly follow the 'Point' interface, TypeScript will throw a compile-time error:

```
// Error: Property 'x' is missing in type '{ y: number; }' but
    required in type 'Point'.
const pointC: Point = { y: 5 };
```

In short, interfaces in TypeScript are powerful tools that help us define and enforce structured data within a codebase, improving the maintainability, and reliability of the code. They are especially helpful in the context of large projects, where enforcing contracts becomes crucial for long-term success.

Here's a small chart demonstrating the concept of interfaces:

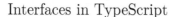

Interfaces in TypeScript

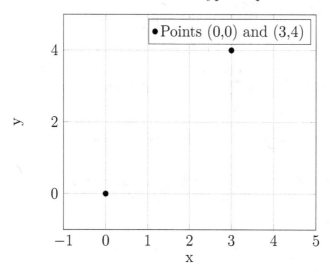

In this chart, we visualize the points defined in our example, representing the two-dimensional space where the points 'pointA' and 'pointB' are located. The interface 'Point' would define the structure for any 'x' and 'y' values within this space.

2.7   How does TypeScript handle null and undefined values?

TypeScript handles 'null' and 'undefined' values as special types, distinct from other types in the type system. However, by default, TypeScript allows assigning 'null' and 'undefined' to any type, which can lead to some unintended behavior.

To illustrate the basic behavior of 'null' and 'undefined'
in TypeScript, consider the following example:

```
let str: string = "Hello, world!";
str = null; // No error
str = undefined; // No error
```

In the above example, although the variable 'str' has a
type of 'string', TypeScript allows assigning 'null' and
'undefined' to it without throwing any error.

However, TypeScript provides a strict null checking feature, which can be enabled by setting the 'strictNullChecks'
flag in the 'tsconfig.json' configuration file or adding the
'–strictNullChecks' flag to the compiler options.

When strict null checks are enabled, TypeScript enforces
stricter rules around assignments and checks involving
'null' and 'undefined'. Here's an example demonstrating
this behavior:

```
let str: string = "Hello, world!";
str = null; // Error: Type 'null' is not assignable to type 'string'

str = undefined; // Error: Type 'undefined' is not assignable to
    type 'string'
```

Now, to work with strict null checks, you should use union
types to explicitly allow 'null' and 'undefined' values:

```
let str: string | null | undefined = "Hello, world!";
str = null; // No error
str = undefined; // No error
```

With strict null checks enabled, TypeScript improves type

safety and helps eliminate the possibility of runtime errors
caused by unintended 'null' or 'undefined' values.

Additionally, TypeScript provides two utility types 'Non-
Nullable<T>' and 'Required<T>' that help in stricter
type checking. The 'NonNullable<T>' type removes 'null'
and 'undefined' from the given type, while 'Required<T>'
makes all properties of the type required and removes 'undefined'.

To better understand how TypeScript uses these types,
consider the following code snippet:

```
type Person = {
  name: string | null;
  age: number | undefined;
}

type NonNullablePerson = NonNullable<Person>; // Error: Property '
    age' is optional in type 'Person' but required in type '
    Required<Person>'

type RequiredPerson = Required<Person>;
const person: RequiredPerson = {
  name: "John",
  age: 30
};
person.age = undefined; // Error: Type 'undefined' is not
    assignable to type 'number'
```

In conclusion, TypeScript handles 'null' and 'undefined'
values as distinct types by default; however, it allows them
to be assigned to any type. By enabling strict null checks
in TypeScript, the type system will force developers to
handle 'null' and 'undefined' values explicitly and improve
the type safety of the code.

2.8 How do you define and call a function in TypeScript?

In TypeScript, you can define a function using the 'function' keyword followed by the function name, parameters in parentheses, and a return type after a colon. The function body is enclosed in curly braces ".

Here's an example of a function definition in TypeScript:

```
function add(a: number, b: number): number {
  return a + b;
}
```

In this example, we've defined a function called 'add' which takes two parameters 'a' and 'b' of type 'number' and returns a value of type 'number'.

To call a function in TypeScript, you use the function name followed by the arguments within parentheses. Here's how you can call the 'add' function:

```
const result = add(3, 4);
console.log(result); // Output: 7
```

This function call passes '3' and '4' as arguments to the 'add' function and stores the return value in the 'result' variable.

Here's a complete example in TypeScript:

```
function add(a: number, b: number): number {
  return a + b;
}
```

```
const result = add(3, 4);
console.log(result); // Output: 7
```

The function definition and call is represented as follows:

Function Definition:

$$\text{function add}(a : \mathbb{N}, b : \mathbb{N}) : \mathbb{N}\{ \quad \text{return } a + b; \} \quad (2.1)$$

Function Call:

$$\text{const result} = \text{add}(3, 4); \qquad (2.2)$$

2.9   Can you explain the concept of 'classes' in TypeScript and how it supports Object-Oriented Programming (OOP)?

In TypeScript, a class is a blueprint for creating objects that share similar properties and methods. It is a fundamental concept in Object-Oriented Programming (OOP) and provides a way to encapsulate data and behavior within a single entity.

TypeScript classes support features like inheritance, interfaces, access modifiers, method overloading, and static properties. These help in creating more structured and reusable code.

Let's break down the main features of TypeScript classes and how they support OOP principles.

1. Encapsulation:

Encapsulation is the concept of bundling data (properties) and operations (methods) within a single unit, the class. This makes it possible to restrict access to certain properties and methods, ensuring a consistent state for the object.

In TypeScript, you can create a class using the 'class' keyword, followed by the class name:

```
class Person {
    private name: string;
    private age: number;

    constructor(name: string, age: number) {
        this.name = name;
        this.age = age;
    }

    public sayHello(): string {
        return `Hello, my name is ${this.name} and I am ${this.age}
            years old.`;
    }
}
```

2. Inheritance:

Inheritance allows a class (the derived class) to inherit properties and methods from another class (the base class). This promotes the principle of reusability in OOP.

In TypeScript, you can use the 'extends' keyword for inheritance:

```
class Employee extends Person {
    private role: string;
```

```
constructor(name: string, age: number, role: string) {
    super(name, age); // call the base class's constructor
    this.role = role;
}

public getRole(): string {
    return this.role;
}
}
```

3. Abstraction and Interfaces:

Abstraction is the process of defining a contract for a class while leaving the implementation details to the derived classes. In TypeScript, you can achieve this using interfaces or abstract classes.

Interfaces define a contract that a class must implement, and TypeScript enforces this contract during compilation:

```
interface IPayroll {
    calculateSalary(): number;
}

class FullTimeEmployee extends Employee implements IPayroll {
    private salary: number;

    constructor(name: string, age: number, role: string, salary:
        number) {
        super(name, age, role);
        this.salary = salary;
    }

    public calculateSalary(): number {
        return this.salary;
    }
}
```

Abstract classes allow you to create methods or properties that must be implemented or overridden in a derived class:

```
abstract class Animal {
    abstract makeSound(): string;
```

```
}
class Dog extends Animal {
    public makeSound(): string {
        return 'Woof!';
    }
}
```

4. Polymorphism:

Polymorphism enables multiple implementations of a method with the same name in different classes or in derived classes. In TypeScript, you can achieve polymorphism with method overriding and interfaces:

```
class PartTimeEmployee extends Employee implements IPayroll {
    private hourlyRate: number;
    private hoursWorked: number;

    constructor(name: string, age: number, role: string, hourlyRate
        : number, hoursWorked: number) {
        super(name, age, role);
        this.hourlyRate = hourlyRate;
        this.hoursWorked = hoursWorked;
    }

    public calculateSalary(): number {
        return this.hourlyRate * this.hoursWorked;
    }
}
```

In the example above, both 'FullTimeEmployee' and 'PartTimeEmployee' implement the 'IPayroll' interface and provide their own implementation for the 'calculateSalary' method.

In summary, TypeScript classes provide a powerful way to model real-world objects using OOP principles like encapsulation, inheritance, abstraction, and polymorphism. They help in organizing code, making it more modular, reusable, and maintainable.

2.10   What are 'enums' in Type-Script and how can you use them?

'Enums' in TypeScript is a feature that allows you to define a named set of constant values, typically to represent a collection of related items or categories. Enums can make your code more understandable and less error-prone by providing a way to use symbolic names rather than raw values, such as integers or strings, directly.

There are two main types of enums in TypeScript: numeric enums and string enums.

1. Numeric enums:

By default, numeric enums will have their members' values auto-incremented from 0. You can also explicitly set the initial value or assign specific values to each member.

Example:

```
enum DaysOfWeek {
  Sunday,    // 0
  Monday,    // 1
  Tuesday,   // 2
  Wednesday, // 3
  Thursday,  // 4
  Friday,    // 5
  Saturday   // 6
}
```

Usage:

```
const today: DaysOfWeek = DaysOfWeek.Friday;
console.log(today); // 5
```

2. String enums:

These Enums allow you to use string values instead of numeric values.

Example:

```
enum Directions {
  Up = "UP",
  Down = "DOWN",
  Left = "LEFT",
  Right = "RIGHT"
}
```

Usage:

```
const move: Directions = Directions.Left;
console.log(move); // "LEFT"
```

Enums in TypeScript are a feature that allows you to define a named set of constant values, typically to represent a collection of related items or categories. Enums can make your code more understandable and less error-prone by providing a way to use symbolic names rather than raw values, such as integers or strings, directly.

There are two main types of enums in TypeScript: numeric enums and string enums.

1. Numeric enums:

By default, numeric enums will have their members' values auto-incremented from 0. You can also explicitly set the initial value or assign specific values to each member.

Example:

```
enum DaysOfWeek {
  Sunday,   // 0
  Monday,   // 1
  Tuesday,  // 2
  Wednesday, // 3
  Thursday, // 4
  Friday,   // 5
  Saturday  // 6
}
```

Usage:

```
const today: DaysOfWeek = DaysOfWeek.Friday;
console.log(today); // 5
```

2. String enums:

These enums allow you to use string values instead of numeric values.

Example:

```
enum Directions {
  Up = "UP",
  Down = "DOWN",
  Left = "LEFT",
  Right = "RIGHT"
}
```

Usage:

```
const move: Directions = Directions.Left;
console.log(move); // "LEFT"
```

2.11 What are generics in TypeScript and why are they useful?

Generics in TypeScript are a way to create reusable and flexible components that can work with multiple types. They are useful because they let you create reusable code that can accept a variety of input types without sacrificing type safety.

When we write code, we often encounter situations where we need to perform the same operation on different types of data. To handle these cases without generics, we could either write separate functions for each data type, or use a less type-safe approach with the 'any' type. The former leads to code duplication, while the latter sacrifices valuable type information.

Generics solve this problem by allowing us to create functions, classes, and interfaces that work with a placeholder type, which is later substituted with the actual data type when the code is invoked. This way, we can have a single implementation that works with different types, while maintaining type safety.

Let's look at an example to illustrate generics. Suppose you want to create a function 'identity' that simply returns its input value:

```
function identity<T>(arg: T): T {
  return arg;
```

```
    }
```

Here, 'T' is the generic type parameter, representing the
input and output type of the 'identity' function. Now we
can use this function with various types:

```
// The explicit way to provide the type argument
const numberIdentity = identity<number>(42);
const stringIdentity = identity<string>('Hello,␣TypeScript!');

// The TypeScript compiler can infer the type argument
const booleanIdentity = identity(true);
```

The generic function 'identity' can be represented as:

$$\forall T \Rightarrow \text{identity} : T \to T$$

In this case, the generic type 'T' is universally quantified,
meaning it can be any type. When we call the 'identity'
function with a specific type, the generic type 'T' is replaced with the actual type, maintaining complete type
information.

Generics are also useful in classes and interfaces, providing generalized behavior that can be flexibly applied to
different types.

Here's an example of a generic 'Stack' class:

```
class Stack<T> {
  private items: T[] = [];

  push(item: T): void {
    this.items.push(item);
  }
```

```
pop(): T | undefined {
  return this.items.pop();
}
}
```

The 'Stack' class can now be instantiated for specific types, such as:

```
const numberStack = new Stack<number>();
numberStack.push(42);
const poppedNumber = numberStack.pop(); // Typed as `number |
    undefined`

const stringStack = new Stack<string>();
stringStack.push('Hello,␣TypeScript!');
const poppedString = stringStack.pop(); // Typed as `string |
    undefined`
```

In summary, generics in TypeScript provide a means of writing reusable and type-safe code that can work with multiple data types. They enable the creation of flexible functions, classes, and interfaces, reducing code duplication and preserving valuable type information throughout our applications.

2.12   What are modules in Type-Script and how do they help in organizing code?

Modules in TypeScript are a way to organize and encapsulate code, allowing you to split your code into smaller, more manageable pieces. They help in maintaining large-scale projects by keeping each part of the code in separate

files and exposing only the necessary parts to the rest of
the application. They promote code reusability, maintainability, and keep the global scope clean, preventing
naming conflicts.

In TypeScript, a module is a file containing statements
and declarations, which can export or import values from
other modules. There are two main types of modules
in TypeScript: namespace modules (or internal modules)
and external modules.

1. Namespace Modules:

These were previously called "internal modules" but are
now called "namespaces.". They use the 'namespace' keyword to create a single, top-level module with multiple
nested modules inside.

```
namespace MyNamespace {
    export class MyClass {
        constructor() {
            console.log("Hello from MyClass in MyNamespace");
        }
    }
}

let example = new MyNamespace.MyClass();
```

Namespace modules are not commonly used nowadays, as
they have been mostly replaced by external modules when
working with modern module bundlers.

2. External Modules:

External modules are the most common way to work with
modules in TypeScript. These are simply regular Type-

Script files that use the 'import' and 'export' keywords to share code between files. The module format is determined by the 'module' setting in the 'tsconfig.json' file (e.g., CommonJS, ES2015, AMD, System). Here's an example:

'math.ts':

```
export function add(a: number, b: number): number {
    return a + b;
}
```

'main.ts':

```
import { add } from "./math";

console.log(add(1, 2));
```

In this example, the 'add' function is exported from the 'math.ts' file and then imported into the 'main.ts' file. The code stays organized by keeping related functions and classes in separate files.

To summarize, TypeScript modules provide a way to organize your code in a clean and structured manner, making it easier to maintain and share between different parts of your application. They prevent naming conflicts and ensure code reusability.

2.13   How can you define an array in TypeScript?

In TypeScript, you can define an array in multiple ways. Here are the three most common methods to define an array:

1. Using square bracket '[]' notation:

```
let arr1: number[] = [1, 2, 3, 4, 5];
let arr2: string[] = ['one', 'two', 'three', 'four', 'five'];
```

2. Using generic 'Array' type notation:

```
let arr3: Array<number> = [1, 2, 3, 4, 5];
let arr4: Array<string> = ['one', 'two', 'three', 'four', 'five'];
```

3. Using an angle-bracket type assertion:

```
let arr5 = <number[]>[1, 2, 3, 4, 5];
let arr6 = <Array<string>>['one', 'two', 'three', 'four', 'five'];
```

All of these methods create and define an array with specified types. It's usually recommended to use the first or the second way because they are more explicit and, in the case of the first one, more concise.

Here is a comparison table of these array definition methods:

Notation Type	Syntax	Example
Square Bracket	dataType[]	let arr: number[] = [1, 2, 3];
Generic Array	Array<dataType>	let arr: Array<number> = [1, 2, 3];
Angle-Bracket Type Assertion	<dataType[]>	let arr = <number[]>[1, 2, 3];

When working with multidimensional arrays, you can define them as follows:

```
// Two-dimensional array of numbers
let matrix: number[][] = [
    [1, 2, 3],
    [4, 5, 6],
    [7, 8, 9]
];
```

In this example, the type 'number[][]' denotes a two-dimensional array of numbers. You can do the same with other data types and other dimensions.

2.14   What are 'tuples' in TypeScript?

In TypeScript, a tuple is a special array-like data structure that allows you to store values of different types with a fixed number of elements. You can define a tuple by providing the types of its elements in a specific order within square brackets, separated by commas. Once you declare the types of the elements, the order becomes important, and you cannot add more elements than the defined tuple length.

Here is an example of a tuple in TypeScript:

```
let tupleExample: [string, number, boolean];
tupleExample = ["TypeScript", 2021, true]; // This is a valid
    tuple assignment
```

In this example, 'tupleExample' is defined to have exactly three elements: a 'string', a 'number', and a 'boolean'. The order of these elements in the tuple is important. For example, if you try to assign different types in a different order, TypeScript will throw a compile-time error:

```
tupleExample = [2021, "TypeScript", true]; // This would cause a
    compile-time error
```

Another feature of tuples in TypeScript is that you can access and manipulate their elements using indexing, just like you would do with regular arrays:

```
console.log(tupleExample[0]); // Output: "TypeScript"
tupleExample[1] = 2022; // Update the number value in the tuple
```

However, you cannot add more elements to a tuple than its declared length:

```
tupleExample[3] = "New element"; // This would cause a compile-
    time error
```

In summary, tuples in TypeScript provide a way to define fixed-length, ordered collections of values with different types, enabling strict compile-time checks on the structure of the data being represented.

2.15 How does TypeScript support optional parameters in function?

TypeScript supports optional parameters in functions by allowing you to specify a question mark '¿ after the parameter name. When a parameter is marked as optional, it means that you can omit that parameter when calling the function, and if it is not provided, it will be assigned the value 'undefined'.

Here's an example:

```
function greet(name: string, age?: number): string {
    if (age === undefined) {
        return `Hello, ${name}!`;
    } else {
        return `Hello, ${name}! You are ${age} years old.`;
    }
}
```

In this example, the 'age' parameter is marked as optional with the '¿ symbol. This means that you can call the 'greet' function with one or two arguments:

```
console.log(greet("John"));          // Output: Hello, John!
console.log(greet("John", 25));      // Output: Hello, John! You
                                     //    are 25 years old.
```

You can also use default parameter values in TypeScript functions. Default values allow you to specify a default value for an optional parameter. If the parameter is not provided, the function will use the default value you specified. Here's an example using default values:

```
function greetWithDefault(name: string, age: number = 30): string
    {
    return `Hello, ${name}! You are ${age} years old.`;
}
```

Now, if you omit the 'age' parameter when calling the
'greetWithDefault' function, it will use the default value
of '30':

```
console.log(greetWithDefault("John")); // Output: Hello, John! You
    are 30 years old.
console.log(greetWithDefault("John", 25)); // Output: Hello, John!
    You are 25 years old.
```

In summary, TypeScript supports optional parameters by
using the ? symbol after a parameter's name and by allowing you to provide default values for optional parameters.
This enables you to create more flexible functions that
can be called with varying numbers of arguments.

2.16   What is 'any' type in Type-Script and when should you use it?

In TypeScript, the 'any' type is a supertype that represents any possible JavaScript value. This type is used
when you don't want to restrict a variable or parameter to
any specific type or when you don't have enough type information available. It essentially bypasses TypeScript's
type checker, enabling you to work with a variable without worrying about its constraints.

Using the 'any' type can be useful in certain situations, but it can also lead to issues down the road, as you lose the benefits of TypeScript's type checking system. It is generally not recommended to use it frequently, since it defeats the purpose of using TypeScript for better type safety and error checking.

Here's a simple example that demonstrates the use of 'any' type:

```
function logValue(value: any): void {
    console.log(value);
}

logValue(42);       // number
logValue("Hello"); // string
logValue({a: 1, b: 2});// object
```

As for when to use the 'any' type, you should use it sparingly and only when absolutely necessary. Some appropriate use cases include:

1. Working with third-party libraries that lack proper type definitions. 2. Gradual migration from JavaScript to TypeScript where you don't have full type information for the entire codebase. 3. Dealing with complex or dynamic data types, where creating an exact type definition might be tedious or difficult.

However, it's often better to use other TypeScript features, like Union Types or Type Guards, to handle complex or dynamic data types more precisely.

Finally, here's a simple flowchart that can help you decide whether to use the 'any' type (**Yes** branches indicate that you should consider using **any**, whereas the **No** branches demonstrate that other solutions should be pursued):

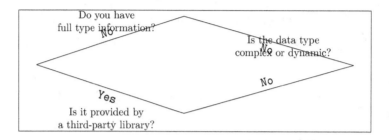

In conclusion, the 'any' type in TypeScript is a powerful and flexible utility that allows you to work with values of unknown or arbitrary types. However, it should be used with caution and only when other, more appropriate TypeScript features are insufficient, as it can lead to weaker type safety and error checking.

2.17   How would you perform Type Assertion in TypeScript?

Type Assertion in TypeScript is a way to hint to the compiler that you know more about a particular value's type than the type inference system does. Type assertion allows you to explicitly specify the type of a value, and it is a way of telling the TypeScript compiler that you are certain about the type of a variable or expression.

There are two ways to perform type assertion in Type-

Script:

1. Using angle-bracket syntax:

```
let value: any = "This is a string";
let strLength: number = (<string>value).length;
```

2. Using the 'as' keyword:

```
let value: any = "This is a string";
let strLength: number = (value as string).length;
```

In both cases, you are asserting that the value has the specified type (in this case, 'string'). Note that this operation does not perform any runtime type checks or conversions; it only serves as a hint to the TypeScript compiler.

Here's an example with a shape interface and a function to calculate its area with type assertion:

```
interface Circle {
    kind: "circle";
    radius: number;
}

interface Square {
    kind: "square";
    sideLength: number;
}

type Shape = Circle | Square;

function getArea(shape: Shape): number {
    if (shape.kind === "circle") {
        return Math.PI * (shape as Circle).radius ** 2;
    } else {
        return (shape as Square).sideLength ** 2;
    }
}
```

In this example, we use type assertion to inform the TypeScript compiler that 'shape' is a 'Circle' or 'Square' based on its 'kind' property.

It's important to note that type assertion should be used with caution, as it can lead to runtime errors if used improperly or excessively. Use type assertion only when you are sure about the value's type, and it's not feasible for the TypeScript compiler to infer it.

2.18   What is 'never' type in TypeScript and what is its purpose?

The 'never' type in TypeScript represents a value that should never happen. This type is primarily used in situations where the code should never reach this point, such as during exhaustive checks, unreachable endpoints, or infinite loops.

The purpose of the 'never' type is to ensure type safety in situations where a value should not exist or should not be accessible. When a function or a variable is expected to have a 'never' type, it indicates to TypeScript that the code should not reach this point, and therefore, it should issue a compile-time error if the code tries to access this value.

Here are some examples of 'never' type usage:

1. Functions that throw errors:

```
function error(message: string): never {
    throw new Error(message);
}
```

In this case, the 'error' function takes a string as an argument and throws an error. The function is expected to
return a 'never' type, which means it should not have a
return value.

2. Functions with infinite loops:

```
function infiniteLoop(): never {
    while (true) {
    }
}
```

In this case, the 'infiniteLoop' function contains an infinite
loop that never terminates. The function is expected to
return a 'never' type, which means it should not have a
return value.

3. Exhaustive type checking:

```
type UnionType = 'typeA' | 'typeB';

function exhaustiveCheck(value: UnionType): never {
    throw new Error(`Unhandled value: ${value}`);
}

function handleUnionType(value: UnionType) {
    switch (value) {
        case 'typeA':
            return 'Handled type A';
        case 'typeB':
            return 'Handled type B';
        default:
            return exhaustiveCheck(value);
    }
}
```

In this case, the 'UnionType' is a union of different string literals, and the 'handleUnionType' function handles each possible value of the 'UnionType'. If any unhandled value is passed to the function, it calls the 'exhaustiveCheck' function, which is expected to return a 'never' type, ensuring that the TypeScript compiler will raise an error if there is any unhandled value.

Using the 'never' type allows TypeScript to identify unreachable code segments, improper type handling, or potential issues in the code, thus improving the overall type safety of the codebase.

2.19   What is 'strict null checks' in TypeScript and how does it help?

In TypeScript, 'strict null checks' is a compiler option that enforces stricter type checking rules. When this option is enabled, the types 'null' and 'undefined' are treated as distinct types from every other type, making it impossible to inadvertently use them in an unsafe manner. The strict null checks option can be activated by adding the '"strictNullChecks": true' flag to the 'tsconfig.json' file or using the '–strictNullChecks' command line flag with the TypeScript compiler.

The objective of strict null checks is to catch potential bugs and improve the safety of your TypeScript code.

Let's see how it works and why it is useful with some examples:

1. Without strict null checks:

```
function greet(name: string) {
  return `Hello, ${name}!`;
}

const user: string = null;
console.log(greet(user)); // TypeError: Cannot read property '
    toUpperCase' of null
```

Here, since the 'user' is 'null', at runtime you would get an error, but TypeScript doesn't show an error at the compile-time because it considers the 'null' to be a valid value for type 'string'. This may lead to undetected bugs in your code.

2. With strict null checks:

```
function greet(name: string) {
  return `Hello, ${name}!`;
}

const user: string = null; // Error: Type 'null' is not assignable
    to type 'string'.
console.log(greet(user));
```

When using strict null checks, TypeScript will report an error when trying to assign 'null' to a variable of type 'string'. This helps you detect and fix potential null-related issues early, before the code runs.

To further illustrate the benefit of strict null checks, let's take more complex example. We define a type 'Person' and a function 'getPersonAge':

```
type Person = {
```

```
  name: string;
  age: number;
};

function getPersonAge(person: Person): number {
  return person.age;
}

const person: Person = null;
console.log(getPersonAge(person)); // RuntimeError: Cannot read
      property 'age' of null
```

Without strict null checks, we encounter the same problem as before - this code would give an error at runtime, but TypeScript wouldn't catch it at the compile-time.

But when we enable strict null checks, TypeScript shows an error at the line of assigning 'null' to 'person':

```
const person: Person = null; // Error: Type 'null' is not
      assignable to type 'Person'
```

Now, we are forced to provide a valid 'Person' object or handle the 'null' case explicitly. This guarantees that we don't run into runtime errors caused by undefined or null values.

In general, strict null checks help you create more robust and safer TypeScript code, making it easier to identify and handle potential issues related to 'null' and 'undefined' values. By enforcing strict typing, it encourages you to write clearer and more predictable code, reducing the likelihood of errors and simplifying debugging.

2.20 What are access modifiers in TypeScript and what are their roles in class properties and methods?

Access modifiers in TypeScript are keywords that determine the visibility and accessibility of class members (properties and methods). There are three access modifiers available in TypeScript:

1. Public

2. Private

3. Protected

By default, all class members are assumed to be public if no access modifier is specified.

Let's discuss each of these access modifiers with their roles in class properties and methods.

1. 'public': The 'public' modifier allows a class member (property or method) to be accessible everywhere. You can access a public member within the class itself, in derived classes, and anywhere outside the class.

Here's an example:

```
class MyClass {
  public property: number;

  public method(): void {
```

```
    console.log("This is a public method.");
  }
}

const obj = new MyClass();

// Accessible outside the class
obj.property = 5;
obj.method();
```

2. 'private': The 'private' modifier restricts access to the class member to within the class itself. This means that you cannot access a private property or method from derived classes or outside the class.

Example:

```
class MyClass {
  private property: number;

  private method(): void {
    console.log("This is a private method.");
  }
}

const obj = new MyClass();

// Not accessible outside the class
// obj.property = 5; // Error: Property 'property' is private and
    only accessible within class 'MyClass'.
// obj.method(); // Error: Property 'method' is private and only
    accessible within class 'MyClass'.
```

3. 'protected': The 'protected' modifier is similar to 'private'. A protected class member is only accessible within the class and any derived classes. This means that you cannot access a protected member from outside the class.

Example:

```
class MyClass {
  protected property: number;

  protected method(): void {
```

```
    console.log("This is a protected method.");
  }
}

class DerivedClass extends MyClass {
  public printPropertyAndMethod(): void {
    console.log("Property:", this.property);
    this.method();
  }
}

const obj = new DerivedClass();

// Accessible in the derived class
obj.printPropertyAndMethod();

// Not accessible outside the class
// obj.property = 5; // Error: Property 'property' is protected and
     only accessible within class 'MyClass' and its subclasses.
// obj.method(); // Error: Property 'method' is protected and only
     accessible within class 'MyClass' and its subclasses.
```

In conclusion, access modifiers in TypeScript play an important role in determining the accessibility and visibility of class members. They help encapsulate and manage the internal state and behavior of a class.

Chapter 3

Intermediate

3.1 Can you explain the differences between 'let', 'const', and 'var' in TypeScript?

In TypeScript (as well as JavaScript ES6+), 'let', 'const', and 'var' are used to declare variables. They have different scoping rules and behavior, which I will explain in detail.

1. 'var':

When using 'var', the variable is function-scoped or globally scoped, depending on where it is declared. When a variable is declared using 'var', it is "hoisted" to the top of its scope. Hoisting means that the variable declaration is moved to the top of the scope, but the assignment of the variable's value remains in its original position.

Here's an example illustrating hoisting:

```
function exampleFunction() {
    console.log(variable); // Output: undefined
    var variable = 5;
    console.log(variable); // Output: 5
}
```

In this example, the variable declaration 'var variable' is hoisted to the top of the function, but the assignment 'variable = 5' remains in its position. So, the code is executed as if it were written like this:

```
function exampleFunction() {
    var variable;
    console.log(variable); // Output: undefined
    variable = 5;
    console.log(variable); // Output: 5
}
```

2. 'let':

The 'let' keyword is used for declaring variables that are block-scoped, meaning their scope is limited to the nearest enclosing block, such as a loop or conditional statement. Unlike 'var', variables declared with 'let' are not hoisted, they also cannot be re-declared within the same scope.

Below is an example comparing variables declared with 'let' and 'var':

```
function exampleFunction() {
    var localVar1 = 1;
    let localVar2 = 2;

    if (true) {
        var localVar1 = 3; // localVar1 is re-assigned
```

```
    let localVar2 = 4; // localVar2 is declared within the new
        block scope

    console.log(localVar1); // Output: 3
    console.log(localVar2); // Output: 4
}

console.log(localVar1); // Output: 3
console.log(localVar2); // Output: 2
}
```

3. 'const': The 'const' keyword, similar to 'let', is block-scoped. The difference, however, is that variables declared with 'const' cannot be re-assigned after they have been initialized, making them constant values.

Here's an example using the 'const' keyword:

```
function exampleFunction() {
    const localVar = 1;

    if (true) {
        const localVar = 2; // localVar is declared within the new
            block scope

        console.log(localVar); // Output: 2
    }

    console.log(localVar); // Output: 1
}
```

In summary:

- 'var': function-scoped or globally scoped, can be re-assigned, and hoisted.

- 'let': block-scoped, can be re-assigned, but not hoisted.

- 'const': block-scoped, cannot be re-assigned, and not hoisted.

For best practices, it is recommended to use 'const' when declaring variables that don't need to be re-assigned and

'let' for other scenarios. Avoid using 'var' since it has less
predictable behavior due to hoisting and lack of block-
scoping.

3.2   How does TypeScript support default parameters in functions?

TypeScript, like modern JavaScript versions (ES6/EC-
MAScript 2015), supports default parameters in functions. Default parameter values are assigned to a function's formal parameters when the function is called without providing specific arguments for those parameters.
This can help you write more flexible and concise functions, as well as make your code more readable.

Here's a brief syntax overview of assigning default values
to parameters in TypeScript:

```
function functionName(parameterName: type = defaultValue):
    returnType {
  // function body
}
```

You can assign default values to any number of parameters within a function. Let's look at an example function
with default parameter values:

```
function greet(name: string, greeting: string = 'Hello'): string {
  return `${greeting}, ${name}!`;
}
```

In this example, the function 'greet' takes two parameters: 'name' and 'greeting'. If the 'greeting' parameter is not provided when calling the function, it will default to the string ''Hello''.

Let's see how this works with different function calls:

```
console.log(greet('Alice')); // "Hello, Alice!"
console.log(greet('Bob', 'Hi')); // "Hi, Bob!"
```

When calling 'greet('Alice')', no 'greeting' argument is provided, so the default 'greeting' value ''Hello'' is used in the function body. The output of 'greet('Bob', 'Hi')' is ''Hi, Bob!'', as the 'greeting' argument ''Hi'' is used instead of the default value.

Here's a summary of how default parameters work in TypeScript:

Default parameters in TypeScript:

Default values are assigned to function parameters when the function is called without providing specific arguments for those parameters.

The syntax to specify a default parameter is:

`parameterName: type = defaultValue.`

You can assign default values to any number of parameters within a function.

If a default value is specified for a parameter, it will be used in the function body when that parameter is not explicitly passed during a function call.

3.3 What is the use of namespaces in TypeScript and how do they help in code organization?

Namespaces in TypeScript are a way to organize code and provide a scoped container for different constructs (like classes, interfaces, and functions). They help in structuring the codebase and avoiding naming conflicts, making it easier to maintain the application as it grows.

Using namespaces, you can group your code based on specific functionalities or features, and thus improve code organization and readability.

Here's an example of a namespace in TypeScript:

```
namespace Animals {
  export class Dog {
    constructor(public name: string) {}

    bark() {
      return 'Woof,␣woof!';
    }
  }

  export class Cat {
    constructor(public name: string) {}

    meow() {
      return 'Meow,␣meow!';
    }
  }
```

```
  }
```

In the example above, we've created a 'Animals' namespace that contains 'Dog' and 'Cat' classes. By using the 'export' keyword, we've made these classes accessible from outside the namespace.

To use these classes, you'd refer to them using the namespace:

```
let myDog = new Animals.Dog('Buddy');
console.log(myDog.name); // Output: Buddy
console.log(myDog.bark()); // Output: Woof, woof!

let myCat = new Animals.Cat('Whiskers');
console.log(myCat.name); // Output: Whiskers
console.log(myCat.meow()); // Output: Meow, meow!
```

This example illustrates how namespaces help in keeping the different components of your code organized and scoped, avoiding naming conflicts.

However, it's important to note that with the widespread adoption of ES modules in JavaScript, using modules (which can be imported in a similar way to namespaces) is becoming the preferred way to structure and organize the code.

Here's the previous example using ES modules instead:

```
// animals.ts
export class Dog {
  constructor(public name: string) {}

  bark() {
    return 'Woof,⎵woof!';
  }
}
```

```
export class Cat {
  constructor(public name: string) {}

  meow() {
    return 'Meow,⎵meow!';
  }
}
```

To use these classes, you'd import them using the module
syntax:

```
import { Dog, Cat } from './animals';

let myDog = new Dog('Buddy');
console.log(myDog.name); // Output: Buddy
console.log(myDog.bark()); // Output: Woof, woof!

let myCat = new Cat('Whiskers');
console.log(myCat.name); // Output: Whiskers
console.log(myCat.meow()); // Output: Meow, meow!
```

In summary, namespaces are a way to organize code, avoid
naming conflicts, and provide a scoped container for different constructs in TypeScript. However, ES modules
are becoming the preferred way to structure and organize code, providing similar benefits with a more modern
syntax.

3.4   Can you explain the concept of 'type guards' in TypeScript?

Type guards are a feature in TypeScript that allows you
to narrow down the type of a variable within a conditional
block, ensuring the variable has a specific type. With type
guards, you can write more robust and type-safe code.

In TypeScript, type guards can be created using:

1. 'typeof' type guard

2. 'instanceof' type guard

3. User-defined type guards

Let us discuss these three ways of creating type guards with examples.

1. 'typeof' Type Guard

The 'typeof' type guard is useful when we want to narrow down the type of a variable based on the variable's value.

```
function example(value: string | number): string {
    if (typeof value === "string") {
        // The type of 'value' is narrowed to 'string'
        return `String: ${value.toUpperCase()}`;
    } else {
        // The type of 'value' is narrowed to 'number'
        return `Number: ${value.toFixed(2)}`;
    }
}
```

We use the 'typeof' keyword followed by the value, and then we make an equality comparison to the desired type as a string.

```
text{if }(text{typeof value === "string"}) {
quad text{// The type of 'value' is narrowed to 'string'}
}
```

2. 'instanceof' Type Guard

The 'instanceof' type guard is useful when you want to narrow down the type of a variable based on the variable's instance.

```
class Animal {
    makeSound(): string {
        return "Unknown sound";
    }
}

class Dog extends Animal {
    makeSound(): string {
        return "Woof";
    }
}

class Cat extends Animal {
    makeSound(): string {
        return "Meow";
    }
}

function speak(animal: Animal): string {
    if (animal instanceof Dog) {
        // 'animal' is narrowed from 'Animal' to 'Dog'
        return `Dog says: ${animal.makeSound()}`;
    }
    if (animal instanceof Cat) {
        // 'animal' is narrowed from 'Animal' to 'Cat'
        return `Cat says: ${animal.makeSound()}`;
    }

    return `Animal says: ${animal.makeSound()}`;
}
```

We use the 'instanceof' keyword followed by the variable and the class we want to compare it to.

if (animal instanceof Dog) {
// 'animal' is narrowed from 'Animal' to 'Dog'
}

3. User-defined Type Guards

User-defined type guards allow you to create your own type guard functions to narrow down the types based on custom conditions. The syntax for user-defined type guards is:

```
function isType(value: any): value is Type
```

Here's an example of using a user-defined type guard:

```
interface Bird {
    fly(): string;
    layEggs(): string;
}

interface Fish {
    swim(): string;
    layEggs(): string;
}

function isFish(pet: Fish | Bird): pet is Fish {
    return (pet as Fish).swim !== undefined;
}

function move(pet: Fish | Bird): string {
    if (isFish(pet)) {
        // 'pet' is narrowed from 'Fish | Bird' to 'Fish'
        return pet.swim();
    } else {
        // 'pet' is narrowed from 'Fish | Bird' to 'Bird'
        return pet.fly();
    }
}
```

Here, we use 'pet is Fish' in the function signature, which checks if 'pet' is of type 'Fish'.

function isFish(pet: Fish | Bird): pet is Fish

In summary, type guards in TypeScript help you narrow down the types of variables in conditional blocks using 'typeof', 'instanceof', or user-defined type guards, making your code more robust and type-safe.

3.5   How does TypeScript support asynchronous programming? Can you provide an example using async/await?

TypeScript, being a typed superset of JavaScript, supports asynchronous programming via multiple mechanisms, one of the modern and widely used approaches is using 'async/await'. The 'async' and 'await' keywords allow us to write asynchronous code in a more synchronous and clean manner. This is achieved using Promises in the background.

Here's a brief explanation of 'Promise', 'async', and 'await':

1. **Promise**: A Promise is a JavaScript object representing the eventual completion or failure of an asynchronous operation. It allows attaching callbacks to handle the async return value or exception. A Promise is in one of the following states:

- pending: The initial state; neither fulfilled nor rejected.

- fulfilled: The operation completed successfully, and the promise has a resulting value.

- rejected: The operation failed, and the promise has a reason for the failure.

- settled: The operation completed, whether fulfilled or rejected.

2. **async**: The 'async' keyword is added before a
function to declare it as asynchronous. An async function
returns a 'Promise' object. If the function has a return
value, the 'Promise' will be resolved with that value, otherwise, it's resolved with 'undefined'.

3. **await**: The 'await' keyword is used to wait for a
'Promise' to resolve or reject, allowing the asynchronous
operation to complete before proceeding to the next line
of code. It can only be used within an 'async' function.

Here's a simple example demonstrating the usage of 'async/await'
in TypeScript:

```typescript
// Simulate an async operation, like fetching data from a server
function fetchDataFromServer(): Promise<string> {
    return new Promise((resolve) => {
        setTimeout(() => {
            resolve("Data from the server");
        }, 2000);
    });
}

// A function using async/await to call the async operation
async function processData(): Promise<void> {
    console.log("Fetching data...");
    const data = await fetchDataFromServer(); // Use 'await' to
        wait for the Promise to resolve
    console.log("Data fetched:", data);
}

// Invoke the async function
processData();
```

In the example above:

1. 'fetchDataFromServer' represents an asynchronous operation, like fetching data from a server, and returns a
'Promise' containing the simulated data.

2. 'processData' is declared as an 'async' function. Inside the function, we use the 'await' keyword before 'fetch-DataFromServer()' to wait for the completion of the async operation before moving to the next line of code, for example, to log the received data to the console.

When using this code, the output would be:

```
Fetching data...
(2 seconds pause)
Data fetched: Data from the server
```

To summarize, TypeScript supports asynchronous programming and provides a clean and readable way to handle asynchronous code using 'async/await'. This makes it more convenient to work with Promises and manage the flow of control in asynchronous operations.

3.6   What are decorators in Type-Script and how can you use them?

Decorators in TypeScript are special kind of declarations that can be attached to classes, methods, accessor, property, or parameter. Decorators use the form '@expression', where 'expression' must evaluate to a function that will be called at runtime with information about the decorated declaration. They provide a flexible way to modify or extend the behavior of a class or its members without altering their original source code.

To use decorators in TypeScript, you need to enable the 'experimentalDecorators' compiler option either through the 'tsconfig.json' configuration file or by passing '–experimentalDecorators' flag to the 'tsc' command.

Here's an overview of common types of decorators:

1. Class decorator:

Applied to the class constructor, can be used to observe, modify, or replace a class definition.

Example:

```
function sealed(constructor: Function) {
    Object.seal(constructor);
    Object.seal(constructor.prototype);
}
@sealed
class MyClass {
    // ...
}
```

2. Method decorator:

Applied to the property descriptor for a method, can be used to observe, modify, or replace a method definition.

Example:

```
function log(target: any, propertyKey: string, descriptor:
    PropertyDescriptor) {
    const originalMethod = descriptor.value;

    descriptor.value = function (...args: any[]) {
        console.log(`Called ${propertyKey} with args:`, args);
```

```
        return originalMethod.apply(this, args);
    };

    return descriptor;
}

class MyClass {
    @log
    myMethod(arg1: number, arg2: string) {
        // ...
    }
}
```

3. Accessor decorator:

Applied to the property descriptor for an accessor, can be used to observe, modify, or replace an accessor's getter or setter.

Example:

```
function readonly(target: any, propertyKey: string, descriptor:
    PropertyDescriptor) {
    descriptor.writable = false;
    return descriptor;
}

class MyClass {
    private _field: number;

    @readonly
    get field(): number {
        return this._field;
    }

    set field(value: number) {
        this._field = value;
    }
}
```

4. Property decorator:

Applied to a property's prototype, used to observe that a property has been declared for an instance.

Example:

```
function required(target: any, propertyKey: string) {
    // Add propertyKey to required properties for the target class
}

class MyClass {
    @required
    propertyName: string;
}
```

5. Parameter decorator:

Applied to the function of a class constructor or method declaration.

Example:

```
function validate(target: any, propertyKey: string, parameterIndex
    : number) {
    // Add parameter validation logic
}

class MyClass {
    myMethod(@validate arg1: number, arg2: string) {
        // ...
    }
}
```

Keep in mind that decorators in TypeScript are still an experimental feature and may change in future releases. Always refer to the official TypeScript documentation for the latest information on using decorators.

3.7   How do you handle exceptions in TypeScript? Can you give an example of try/catch/-finally?

In TypeScript, exception handling is done using the 'try', 'catch', and 'finally' constructs, similar to JavaScript. Here's a brief explanation of each construct:

- 'try': Wraps the code that might throw an exception.

- 'catch': Captures the exception thrown by the code inside the 'try' block and contains a block of code to execute when an exception occurs.

- 'finally': Contains a block of code that will always execute regardless of whether an exception occurs or not.

Here's an example illustrating the use of 'try', 'catch', and 'finally':

```
function divide(a: number, b: number): number {
  let result: number;
  try {
    if (b === 0) {
      throw new Error("Division by zero is not allowed");
    }
    result = a / b;
  } catch (error) {
    console.error(`Error: ${error.message}`);
    result = NaN; // return NaN if an error occurs
  } finally {
    console.log("Division operation executed");
  }
  return result;
}

console.log(divide(4, 2)); // 2
```

```
console.log(divide(4, 0)); // NaN


function divide(a: number, b: number): number {
  let result: number;
  try {
    if (b === 0) {
      throw new Error("Division by zero is not allowed");
    }
    result = a / b;
  } catch (error) {
    console.error(`Error: ${error.message}`);
    result = NaN; // return NaN if an error occurs
  } finally {
    console.log("Division operation executed");
  }
  return result;
}

console.log(divide(4, 2)); // 2
console.log(divide(4, 0)); // NaN
```

In this example, the 'divide' function takes two numbers
as input and returns their quotient. Inside the 'try' block,
we check if the divisor is zero and throw an error if it is.
The 'catch' block captures the error, logs its message, and
assigns 'NaN' to the 'result' variable. The 'finally' block
logs a message indicating that the division operation was
executed. The function then returns the result.

3.8   What is the purpose of the 'readonly' modifier in Type-Script?

In TypeScript, the 'readonly' modifier is used to mark a
property or an index signature declaration as read-only.

Once a property is marked as 'readonly', its value cannot be changed after it has been initialized.

There are several reasons why you'd want to use 'readonly' in your code:

1. *Immutability*: The 'readonly' modifier ensures that the value of a property is not modified after initialization. This can help enforce immutability or protect certain properties from being altered.

2. *Error prevention*: Using 'readonly' helps prevent accidental changes to the value of a property, which could lead to bugs or unexpected behavior in your program.

3. *Code clarity*: When a property is marked as 'readonly', it communicates to other developers that the value should not be changed after initialization, making your code more clear and understandable.

Here's an example of how to use the 'readonly' modifier in TypeScript:

```typescript
class Circle {
    readonly pi: number; // Read-only property
    readonly radius: number;

    constructor(radius: number) {
        this.pi = 3.14159265359;
        this.radius = radius;
    }

    area(): number {
        return this.pi * this.radius * this.radius;
    }
}

let circle = new Circle(5);
circle.radius = 10; // Error: Cannot assign to 'radius' because it
    is a read-only property
```

Here, the properties 'pi' and 'radius' are marked as 'read-only', indicating that their values should not be changed after they are initialized in the constructor.

For an array, you can use the 'ReadonlyArray' or 'Readonly<T>'type to create a read-only array:

```
let numbers: ReadonlyArray<number> = [1, 2, 3, 4, 5];
numbers.push(6); // Error: Property 'push' does not exist on type '
    ReadonlyArray<number>'

let moreNumbers: Readonly<number[]> = [1, 2, 3, 4, 5];
moreNumbers[0] = 0; // Error: Index signature in type 'Readonly<
    number[]>' only permits reading
```

In conclusion, the 'readonly' modifier in TypeScript is a useful tool for ensuring immutability and preventing accidental changes to variables or properties in your code, leading to more robust and clear code.

3.9   What is the 'unknown' type in TypeScript and how is it different from 'any' type?

The 'unknown' type is a type-safe counterpart to the 'any' type in TypeScript. While both types can hold any value, there are important differences in how they can be utilized in your code.

'unknown'

With the 'unknown' type, TypeScript enforces type-checking
to make sure the value assigned to an 'unknown' type is
validated before it can be used. To access or use the
value of an 'unknown' type variable, you must first use
type guards, type assertions, or user-defined type guards
to narrow down or assert the specific type you want to
work with.

For example, let's say you have a variable of type 'unknown':

```
let value: unknown;
```

If you try to perform any operation on this variable, Type-
Script will give you a type error:

```
let num: number = value + 1; // Error: Object is of type 'unknown
    '.
```

You must use a type guard or type assertion to narrow
down the type:

```
if (typeof value === "number") {
  let num: number = value + 1; // This is fine now because we
      checked the type
}
```

or

```
let num: number = value as number + 1; // This is fine because we
    asserted the type
```

'any'

On the other hand, the 'any' type can hold any value,
like the 'unknown' type, but it also bypasses TypeScript's

type-checking system. This means you can access properties, call methods, or perform any operation on a variable of type 'any' without TypeScript throwing any errors, even if the operation is incorrect.

For example:

```
let value: any;

value.foo.bar(); // TypeScript won't throw an error
let num: number = value + 1; // TypeScript won't throw an error
```

Summary

While both 'unknown' and 'any' types can hold any value, the main difference is how they affect type checking:

- 'unknown' forces you to perform type-checking or type assertions before accessing or using the value. It ensures that the value doesn't get misused accidentally, which helps maintain type safety in your code.

- 'any' bypasses the type-checking system, allowing you to access or use the value without any restrictions. It could potentially lead to errors at runtime due to incorrect usage.

In most cases, you should prefer using 'unknown' over 'any' to maintain type safety in your TypeScript code.

3.10 How do you create and use a static property in TypeScript?

In TypeScript, a static property is a property that belongs to a class rather than an instance of the class. It means you can access the static property directly from the class itself, rather than from an instance of the class.

To create and use a static property in TypeScript, you can follow these steps:

1. Define a class.

2. Declare a static property using the 'static' keyword.

3. Assign a value to the static property, if you want to initialize it.

4. Access the static property using the syntax '<class-name> .<property-name>'.

Here's an example of how to create and use a static property in TypeScript:

```
class MyClass {
  // Declare and initialize a static property
  static myStaticProperty: number = 42;

  // Regular (non-static) property for comparison
  myInstanceProperty: number;

  constructor(myInstanceProperty: number) {
    this.myInstanceProperty = myInstanceProperty;
  }
}

// Access the static property using the class name
console.log(MyClass.myStaticProperty); // Output: 42

// Access an instance property for comparison
```

```
const instance = new MyClass(24);
console.log(instance.myInstanceProperty); // Output: 24
```

The syntax for declaring and accessing a static property
is as follows:

Declare a static property:

```
static <property-name> : <property-type>;
```

Access a static property:

```
<class-name>.<property-name>
```

3.11   How would you use Type-Script with Node.js?

To use TypeScript with Node.js, you'll need to follow
these steps:

1. **Install Node.js**: If you haven't already, make sure
to have Node.js installed on your system. You can download it from the official website: https://nodejs.org/

2. **Create a new Node.js project**: Open a terminal
or command prompt and create a new directory for your
project. Navigate to the directory and initialize a new
Node.js project by running:

```
mkdir my-ts-node-project
cd my-ts-node-project
npm init -y
```

This will create a default 'package.json' file for your project.

3. **Install TypeScript**: You can install TypeScript globally using the following command:

```
npm install -g typescript
```

Or locally in your project by running:

```
npm install --save-dev typescript
```

4. **Install @types/node**: This package contains type definitions for Node.js, which allows TypeScript to understand how to interact with Node.js APIs. Install it using the following command:

```
npm install --save-dev @types/node
```

5. **Create a tsconfig.json file**: This file configures the TypeScript compiler settings. Create a new 'tsconfig.json' file in the root of your project and add the following configuration:

```
{
  "compilerOptions": {
    "target": "es6",
    "module": "commonjs",
    "strict": true,
    "esModuleInterop": true,
    "outDir": "dist",
    "moduleResolution": "node"
  },
  "include": ["src/**/*.ts"],
  "exclude": ["node_modules"]
}
```

This configuration tells the TypeScript compiler to transpile the '.ts' files in the 'src' directory into JavaScript files in the 'dist' directory. It also specifies that the target JavaScript version should be ES6, and that the module system should use CommonJS (which is what Node.js uses).

6. **Create your TypeScript source files**: Create a new directory named 'src' in your project root, and create a new TypeScript file, e.g., 'index.ts' inside it. Add some code to the 'index.ts' file:

```
const greet = (name: string): string => {
  return `Hello, ${name}!`;
};

console.log(greet("TypeScript"));
```

7. **Add a build and start script**: In your 'package.json' file, add a build script and a start script. The build script will transpile the TypeScript files, and the start script will run the transpiled JavaScript files:

```
"scripts": {
  "build": "tsc",
  "start": "node dist/index.js"
}
```

8. **Build and run your TypeScript code**: In the terminal or command prompt, run the following commands to build and run your code:

```
npm run build
npm run start
```

This will transpile your TypeScript code into JavaScript, and then run the 'dist/index.js' file using Node.js, resulting in the output: 'Hello, TypeScript¡

In conclusion, to use TypeScript with Node.js, you need
to configure your project to use the TypeScript compiler
to transpile your TypeScript code to JavaScript and then
use Node.js to run the transpiled code.

3.12   Can you explain the difference between 'interface' and 'type' in TypeScript?

In TypeScript, both 'interface' and 'type' are used to define custom types. Although they share some similarities, there are fundamental differences between them:

1. Declaration merging: Interfaces support declaration merging, while types do not. This means that you can define multiple interfaces with the same name, and TypeScript will merge them automatically. This can be useful when extending existing interfaces or providing multiple implementations.

Example:

```
interface User {
  firstName: string;
}

interface User {
  lastName: string;
}

// The resulting User interface will have both firstName and
    lastName
With types, if you declare two types with the same name, you'll
    get an error:
```

```
type␣User␣=␣{
␣␣firstName:␣string;
};

type␣User␣=␣{
␣␣lastName:␣string;
};

//␣Error:␣Duplicate␣identifier␣'User'
```

2. Extending and implementing: Interfaces can extend other interfaces using the 'extends' keyword, and classes can implement interfaces using the 'implements' keyword. Types do not support these keywords, but you can achieve similar functionality using intersection types and mapped types.

Interface extending:

```
interface Person {
  name: string;
}

interface Employee extends Person {
  jobTitle: string;
}
```

Type intersection:

```
type Person = {
  name: string;
};

type Employee = Person & {
  jobTitle: string;
};
```

3. Syntax and instantiability: In general, interfaces offer a more flexible and idiomatic way to define structured types, while types are more suited for cases when you need to define union, intersection, or mapped types. However,

some TypeScript constructs, like constructor types, can only be expressed as a 'type', not an 'interface'.

Constructor type example:

```
type Constructable = {
  new (...args: any[]): object;
};
```

4. Introspection and error messages: Types are more powerful in terms of introspection capabilities, like conditional types that can provide more fine-grained control over the resulting type. Additionally, error messages related to type aliases tend to be more informative.

Here's a summary of the differences between 'interface' and 'type' in TypeScript:

Table 3.1: Summary

Property	Interface	Type
Declaration Merging	Yes	No
Extending/Implementing	Extends (for interfaces), Implements (for classes)	Intersection Types
Syntax/Instantiability	Somewhat more convenient for objects	More versatile (unions, etc.)
Introspection/Error	Less powerful/Less informative	More powerful/More informative

In conclusion, 'interface' is recommended for defining structured object types and for type checking, while 'type' should be used for more advanced use cases or when you need additional versatility like union and mapped types.

3.13 How would you create and use an index type in TypeScript?

In TypeScript, an index type is a way to specify that an object should have keys of a specific type and values of another specific type. You can create an index type using square brackets '[]' notation in an interface or a type alias. Let's see an example:

```
interface StringIndexObject {
  [key: string]: number;
}
```

In this example, we created an interface called 'StringIndexObject', in which any object of this type will have keys of type 'string' and values of type 'number'.

Here's an example of how to use this 'StringIndexObject' interface:

```
const myObject: StringIndexObject = {
  a: 1,
  b: 2,
  c: 3,
};

const valueA: number = myObject['a'];
```

Now let's say you want to create an index type for an object with keys of type 'number' and values of type 'string'. Here's how you can do this using a type alias:

```
type NumberIndexObject = {
  [key: number]: string;
};
```

Using this type alias, let's see an example:

```
const myOtherObject: NumberIndexObject = {
  1: "a",
  2: "b",
  3: "c",
};

const valueB: string = myOtherObject[2];
```

In addition, there is a special type in TypeScript called 'keyof' that can be used to create index types based on the keys of another type. Here's an example of how you can use 'keyof' to access the properties of an object:

```
function getProperty<T, K extends keyof T>(obj: T, key: K): T[K] {
  return obj[key];
}

const sampleObject = { a: 1, b: 'hello' };

const numericValue: number = getProperty(sampleObject, 'a');
const stringValue: string = getProperty(sampleObject, 'b');
```

In this example, we're using generic types 'T' and 'K' to create a flexible function that can get a property from various objects of different types. The type 'K' is constrained to be one of the keys of the type 'T', using the 'keyof' keyword. Then, 'T[K]' is used to specify the return type which corresponds to the value type *specific to the key*.

Remember that index types are powerful constructs in TypeScript that make it possible to model the shape and behavior of objects in a more versatile and dynamic way. This allows you to create more robust and type-safe code.

3.14 How do you declare and use a tuple type in TypeScript?

In TypeScript, a tuple is a special type of array where each element can have a specific, predetermined type. Tuples allow you to represent a fixed number of elements having different types, but the types are known at compile time.

To declare a tuple type in TypeScript, you can use the following syntax:

```
type TupleName = [type1, type2, ..., typeN];
```

For example, if you wanted to define a tuple representing a point in 3D space, you could define a tuple type 'Point3D' as follows:

```
type Point3D = [number, number, number];
```

To use a tuple type, you can create a variable of the tuple type and assign values to its elements based on the specified order of types in the definition:

```
let point: Point3D = [1, 2, 3];
```

You may access the elements of tuple using its index, just like you do with a regular array:

```
let x = point[0]; // x will have the value 1
let y = point[1]; // y will have the value 2
let z = point[2]; // z will have the value 3
```

Here's a TypeScript function example that calculates the

Euclidean distance between two 'Point3D' tuples:

```
type Point3D = [number, number, number];

function euclideanDistance(a: Point3D, b: Point3D): number {
    let dx = a[0] - b[0];
    let dy = a[1] - b[1];
    let dz = a[2] - b[2];
    return Math.sqrt(dx * dx + dy * dy + dz * dz);
}

let pointA: Point3D = [1, 2, 3];
let pointB: Point3D = [4, 5, 6];

let distance = euclideanDistance(pointA, pointB);
```

In this example, 'euclideanDistance' is a function that takes two 'Point3D' tuples and returns a 'number'. The distance between the two points is calculated using the Euclidean distance formula:

$$\text{distance} = \sqrt{(x\_1 - x\_2)2 + (y\_1 - y\_2)2 + (z\_1 - z\_2)2}.$$

3.15   How does TypeScript handle optional chaining?

Optional chaining is a feature in TypeScript that allows you to access properties of an object or call a method, even if the object is 'undefined' or 'null'. Instead of throwing an error due to accessing properties of 'undefined' or 'null', it simply returns 'undefined'. TypeScript handles optional chaining using the '?.' operator.

In TypeScript, optional chaining works for properties and methods, as well as function and constructor calls. Here's a brief explanation of each case:

1. **Optional Property Access** When accessing a property, use the '?.' operator to perform an optional property access.

```
const propertyValue = someObject?.property;
```

If 'someObject' is 'undefined' or 'null', 'propertyValue' will be 'undefined'.

2. **Optional Method Access** Similar to properties, you can use the '?.' operator to call a method too.

```
const methodResult = someObject?.method();
```

If 'someObject' is 'undefined' or 'null', or the method does not exist, 'methodResult' will be 'undefined'.

3. **Optional Function Call** When dealing with functions, you can use the '?.()' syntax to make the call optional.

```
const functionResult = someFunction?.();
```

If 'someFunction' is 'undefined' or 'null', 'functionResult' will be 'undefined'.

4. **Optional Constructor Call** When initializing an object using a constructor, use the '?.' operator to make the call optional.

```
const newInstance = SomeClass?.();
```

If 'SomeClass' is 'undefined' or 'null', 'newInstance' will be 'undefined'.

Let's see an example:

```
interface User {
    name: string;
    address?: {
        street: string;
        city: string;
    };
}

const user: User = {
    name: "John",
};

const cityName = user?.address?.city; // Since 'address' is
    missing, 'cityName' will be 'undefined'.
```

In this example, we have defined a 'User' interface with an optional 'address' property. When trying to access the 'city' property, we use optional chaining to avoid errors if the 'address' is not provided. As a result, 'cityName' is assigned the value 'undefined'.

```
User = {
    name: String,
    address?: {
        street: String,
        city: String,
    }
}

user = {
    name: "John",
}

cityName = user?.address?.city // "undefined"
```

3.16 Can you explain the concept of conditional types in TypeScript?

Conditional types are a powerful feature in TypeScript that allows you to express complex type relationships and transformations based on conditions. They can be thought of as a form of type-level logic that makes your type definitions more expressive and flexible.

A conditional type has the following form:

```
T extends U ? X : Y
```

Here, 'T' and 'U' are types, and 'X' and 'Y' are the resulting types. The basic idea is the following:

- If 'T' is assignable to 'U' (i.e., 'T extends U'), then the resulting type is 'X'.
- Otherwise, the resulting type is 'Y'.

Let's take a look at a simple example to illustrate this concept:

```
type IsString<T> = T extends string ? true : false;
```

In this case, we define a conditional type called 'IsString', which checks whether the type 'T' is a 'string'. If it is, the type evaluates to 'true'. Otherwise, it evaluates to 'false'.

Here's how 'IsString' can be used with different types:

```
type A = IsString<string>; // true
type B = IsString<number>; // false
```

Now let's consider a more complex example using conditional types to define a utility type for extracting the return type of a function:

```
type ReturnType<T> = T extends (...args: any[]) => infer R ? R :
    never;
```

Here's a step-by-step explanation of this conditional type:

1. Check if 'T' extends a function type with the form '(...args: any[]) => any'. If it doesn't, the type evaluates to 'never'.

2. If 'T' does extend the function type, use the 'infer' keyword to infer the return type 'R' of the function.

3. If the inference is successful, the type evaluates to 'R'. Otherwise, it evaluates to 'never'.

Let's see how the 'ReturnType' utility type works in practice:

```
type C = ReturnType<() => string>; // string
type D = ReturnType<(x: number, y: number) => boolean>; // boolean
```

The conditional type can be represented as:

$$T \subseteq U \Rightarrow X \,|\, \bar{X} \Rightarrow Y$$

In this formula, T is the tested type, U is the constraint type. If T is assignable to U $(T \subseteq U)$, the resulting type is X. Otherwise, the resulting type is Y.

I hope this explanation helps you understand the concept

of conditional types in TypeScript!

3.17 How does the TypeScript compiler handle ambient declarations or 'd.ts' files?

The TypeScript compiler handles ambient declarations or '.d.ts' files to provide type information about external libraries or code that is either written in vanilla JavaScript or doesn't have its own TypeScript types. These files contain type definitions that enable TypeScript to understand the shapes and types of the external code, making it easier for you to work with them in a type-safe way.

When the TypeScript compiler processes your project, it uses the information provided in '.d.ts' files for type checking and autocompletion functionality in your editor.

Here's a brief overview of how the TypeScript compiler handles '.d.ts' files:

1. **Discovering '.d.ts' files**: The TypeScript compiler discovers '.d.ts' files either through direct references in your code using triple-slash directives ('/// <reference path="..." />'), or by searching for type definition files (usually from the 'node_modules/@types' folder). For instance, when you install a package's type definition as a separate package like '@types/lodash', the compiler will

find the '.d.ts' files inside 'node_modules/@types/lodash'.

2. **Parsing '.d.ts' files**: The TypeScript compiler then
parses the '.d.ts' files and builds an internal representation
of the types and interfaces described in those files. Ambient declarations in a '.d.ts' file are wrapped in 'declare'
keywords that tell the TypeScript compiler they are only
providing type information and not actual implementation.

For example, here's a basic ambient declaration for a function called 'add':

```
declare function add(a: number, b: number): number;
```

This declaration tells the TypeScript compiler that there
exists a function named 'add' that takes two numeric arguments and returns a number. The implementation details are not given, but the TypeScript compiler can use
this information to perform type checking and provide autocompletion suggestions when you use the 'add' function
in your TypeScript code.

3. **Type checking**: With the information gathered
from '.d.ts' files, the TypeScript compiler can perform
type checking on your code that uses those external libraries. This ensures that you are using the correct types
and arguments, as specified by the ambient declarations.

4. **Code generation**: During the compilation process, TypeScript generates JavaScript output. The ambient declarations or '.d.ts' files are not included in the

output JavaScript, as they only contain type information and not actual implementation. The generated JavaScript files will only contain the code written in your TypeScript files.

In summary, the TypeScript compiler uses ambient declarations or '.d.ts' files as a reference for type information of external libraries, allowing you to work with them in a type-safe way. The compiler discovers, parses, and uses these files for type checking and autocompletion, while leaving the implementation details to the external code. The generated JavaScript files contain only code from your TypeScript source files, excluding the type information from '.d.ts' files.

3.18   What are mapped types in TypeScript and how can you use them?

Mapped types in TypeScript are a powerful feature that allows you to create new types based on existing ones by performing transformations on their properties. They essentially enable you to "map" from one type to another by applying a set of rules. Mapped types are useful when you need to make modifications to an existing type, such as making all properties optional or readonly.

A mapped type is defined using a combination of a type

variable, a key 'in' clause, and a mapping expression applied to the properties of the original type. Here's the basic syntax of a mapped type:

```
type MappedType<T> = {
  [P in keyof T]: /* mapping expression based on T[P] */;
};
```

Here, 'P' is a type variable that iterates over all keys of the type 'T'. 'keyof T' is an index type query, which resolves to a union of all property keys of the type 'T'. The mapping expression will be applied to each property value type in 'T', depending on 'T[P]'.

Let's see some examples.

1. **Making all properties of a type optional:**

```
type Partial<T> = {
  [P in keyof T]?: T[P];
};
```

Now, you can create a new type with all properties optional:

```
interface Person {
  name: string;
  age: number;
}

type OptionalPerson = Partial<Person>;
```

Here, 'OptionalPerson' would have the type ' name?: string; age?: number '.

2. **Making all properties of a type readonly:**

```
type Readonly<T> = {
  readonly [P in keyof T]: T[P];
};
```

Then, you can create a new type with all properties readonly:

```
interface Point {
  x: number;
  y: number;
}

type ReadonlyPoint = Readonly<Point>;
```

Now, 'ReadonlyPoint' would have the type ' readonly x: number; readonly y: number '.

3. **Mapping property value types:**

You can also transform the value types of a type, for example, wrapping them in a 'Promise':

```
type PromiseType<T> = {
  [P in keyof T]: Promise<T[P]>;
};
```

Using the 'Point' type from the previous example:

```
type PromisePoint = PromiseType<Point>;
```

In this case, 'PromisePoint' would have the type ' x: Promise<number>; y: Promise<number> '.

You can use mapped types to create powerful utility types and, as they are generic, they can be reused across your codebase. Various mapped types (like 'Partial' and 'Readonly') are already included in TypeScript's standard library for your convenience.

3.19   How do you create a private constructor in TypeScript and why would you want to do it?

In TypeScript, you can create a private constructor by marking the 'constructor' with the 'private' keyword. A class with a private constructor cannot be instantiated from outside the class directly. The main reason for using a private constructor is to apply the Singleton pattern to ensure that a class has only one single instance throughout the lifetime of an application. Here's an example of a class with a private constructor:

```
class Singleton {
  private static instance: Singleton;

  private constructor() {
    // Initialization code
  }

  public static getInstance(): Singleton {
    if (!Singleton.instance) {
      Singleton.instance = new Singleton();
    }
    return Singleton.instance;
  }
}
```

In this example, we have a Singleton class with a private constructor. To create an instance of the Singleton class, we use the static method 'getInstance()'. This method checks if an instance of the Singleton class already exists, and if not, it creates a new instance. Since the 'constructor' is private, we cannot instantiate this class using the 'new' keyword outside of the class, which helps ensure that there's only one instance of the class.

```
class Singleton {
  private static instance: Singleton;

  private constructor() {
    % Initialization code
  }

  public static getInstance(): Singleton {
    if (!Singleton.instance) {
      Singleton.instance = new Singleton();
    }
    return Singleton.instance;
  }
}
```

As for why you would want to use a private constructor, the main reasons are:

1. Singleton pattern: To enforce that a class should have only one instance throughout the lifetime of your application (useful for centralized management, like configuration or logging).

2. Factory pattern: To provide a consistent interface or to create instances of different derived classes based on some criteria, without exposing the constructor directly to the users of the class.

3. Preventing misuse of a class: Restricting the instantiation process so that the class can only be instantiated in specific ways, like through static methods or helper

classes.

3.20   Can you explain the concept of 'type inference' in Type-Script?

Type inference is a feature in TypeScript where the compiler automatically determines the data type of a variable or expression based on the information available at the time of compilation. In other words, the TypeScript compiler attempts to understand the type of a value to ensure that your code is type-safe without the need for explicit type annotations.

Type inference can be useful when declaring variables, setting default function parameters, or even determining the return type of a function. In many cases, type inference allows you to write more concise code while still maintaining type safety.

Let's take a look at some examples to illustrate the concept of type inference in TypeScript.

1. Variable declaration:

```
let x = 5; // inferred to have the 'number' type
let y = 'hello'; // inferred to have the 'string' type

// Later in the code.
x = 10; // No errors, since 'x' is inferred to have the 'number'
    type
y = 'world'; // No errors, since 'y' is inferred to have the '
```

string' type

In this example, TypeScript compiler inferred the type of variables 'x' and 'y' based on the values assigned during their declaration.

2. Inferred return type of a function:

```
function sum(a: number, b: number) {
    return a + b;
}
```

In this case, TypeScript is able to infer that the return type of the 'sum' function is also a 'number' because the result of adding two numbers will always be a number.

3. Inferred type from context:

TypeScript also uses context to infer more specific types from wider types. For example:

```
type Animal = {
    species: string;
};

type Dog = Animal & {
    isPet: boolean;
};

function processAnimal(animal: Animal) {
    if ('isPet' in animal) {
        // 'animal' is now inferred to be of type 'Dog'
    }
}
```

In this case, TypeScript understands that inside the 'if' block, 'animal' must be an instance of the 'Dog' type.

Type inference helps you maintain type safety and write

cleaner, more concise code without the need for unnec-
essary explicit typing. However, in some situations, you
might still want to provide explicit types to prevent subtle
bugs or provide better documentation.

Here is a summary of Type Inference in TypeScript:

Type Inference ⇒ Automatic Type Determination

based on   Available Information

Chapter 4

Advanced

4.1 How can you use TypeScript with popular front-end frameworks like React or Angular?

Using TypeScript with popular front-end frameworks like React and Angular can bring many benefits such as type-safety, better code organization, and improved maintainability. In this answer, I will show you how to use Type-Script with both React and Angular.

React and TypeScript

To use TypeScript with React, you need to create a new React project with TypeScript support or add TypeScript to an existing project. Here's how to create a new React project with TypeScript:

1. Install 'create-react-app' if you haven't already:

```
npm install -g create-react-app
```

2. Create a new React project with TypeScript:

```
create-react-app my-app --template typescript
```

This command will create a new React project named 'my-app' with TypeScript support.

To add TypeScript to an existing React project, follow these steps:

1. Install TypeScript and TypeScript type declarations for React and ReactDOM:

```
npm install --save typescript @types/node @types/react @types/
    react-dom
```

2. Rename your '.js' files to '.tsx', and update the 'import' statements to use '.tsx' extension. For example, change:

```
import App from './App';
```

to

```
import App from './App.tsx';
```

3. Create a 'tsconfig.json' file in your project root:

```
{
```

```
"compilerOptions": {
  "target": "es5",
  "lib": [
    "dom",
    "dom.iterable",
    "esnext"
  ],
  "allowJs": true,
  "skipLibCheck": true,
  "esModuleInterop": true,
  "allowSyntheticDefaultImports": true,
  "strict": true,
  "forceConsistentCasingInFileNames": true,
  "module": "esnext",
  "moduleResolution": "node",
  "resolveJsonModule": true,
  "isolatedModules": true,
  "noEmit": true,
  "jsx": "react-jsx"
},
"include": [
  "src"
]
}
```

Now you can use TypeScript in your React components. For example, you can define an interface for the component props:

```
// src/App.tsx
import React from 'react';

interface AppProps {
  title: string;
}

const App: React.FC<AppProps> = ({ title }) => {
  return (
    <div>
      <h1>{title}</h1>
    </div>
  );
};

export default App;
```

Angular and TypeScript

Angular projects are built with TypeScript by default.

When you create a new Angular project using the Angular CLI, TypeScript is already set up and configured for you. Here's how to create a new Angular project with TypeScript:

1. Install the Angular CLI if you haven't already:

```
npm install -g @angular/cli
```

2. Create a new Angular project:

```
ng new my-app
```

This command will automatically create a new Angular project with TypeScript enabled. Your components, services, and other application logic are written in TypeScript files with the '.ts' extension. Here's an example of a simple component in Angular:

```
// src/app/app.component.ts
import { Component } from '@angular/core';

@Component({
  selector: 'app-root',
  templateUrl: './app.component.html',
  styleUrls: ['./app.component.css']
})
export class AppComponent {
  title = 'my-app';
}
```

This is a basic example of how you can use TypeScript with React and Angular. By combining TypeScript with these popular front-end frameworks, you can enhance the development experience, catch errors early, and create more scalable and maintainable applications.

4.2   How do you define and use a union type in TypeScript?

In TypeScript, a union type allows you to define a type that can be one of several types. You can define a union type using the vertical bar '|' between the types you want to create a union of.

Here's an example of defining a union type:

```
type StringOrNumber = string | number;
```

In this example, we've created a type 'StringOrNumber' that can be either a 'string' or a 'number'.

To use a union type, you can apply it to a variable, a function parameter, or a function return type. Here's how to use the 'StringOrNumber' type we defined earlier:

```
function processValue(value: StringOrNumber) {
    if (typeof value === "string") {
        console.log("Processing a string:", value.toUpperCase());
    } else if (typeof value === "number") {
        console.log("Processing a number:", Math.sqrt(value));
    } else {
        // This case should never be reached
        console.log("Unknown value:", value);
    }
}

const input1: StringOrNumber = "Hello, TypeScript!";
const input2: StringOrNumber = 64;

processValue(input1); // Processing a string: HELLO, TYPESCRIPT!
processValue(input2); // Processing a number: 8
```

In this example, we have a function 'processValue' that takes a 'StringOrNumber' parameter. Inside the function, we use a type guard (the 'typeof' check) to determine if the input value is a 'string' or a 'number'. Depending on the type, we perform different operations, such as converting the string to upper case or calculating the square root.

Notice that if you try to assign a value of an incompatible type to a variable with a union type, TypeScript will show a compile-time error:

```
const input3: StringOrNumber = true; // Error: Type 'boolean' is
      not assignable to type 'StringOrNumber'
```

4.3   Can you explain the concept of 'higher order functions' in TypeScript?

Higher-order functions are functions that either take other functions as arguments, return a function as a result, or both. In TypeScript, higher-order functions are commonly used as a means of code abstraction, primarily to keep code modular and reusable. They are an essential aspect of functional programming and are extensively employed in libraries like Lodash or RxJS.

Here's a brief explanation of some key terms:

1. **First-class functions:** When functions are treated as values and can be assigned to variables or passed as

arguments, they are considered first-class functions.

2. **Higher-order functions:** Functions that accept other functions as arguments or return functions as results are called higher-order functions.

Let's go through some examples to better understand higher-order functions in TypeScript:

Example 1: A function that accepts a function as an argument

```
function exampleFunction(value: number, func: (input: number) =>
    number) {
  return func(value);
}

const square = (x: number) => x * x;

console.log(exampleFunction(5, square)); // Output: 25
```

In this example, 'exampleFunction' is a higher-order function because it accepts a function 'func' as an argument.

Example 2: A function that returns another function

```
function createMultiplier(factor: number): (input: number) =>
    number {
  return (x: number) => x * factor;
}

const double = createMultiplier(2);

console.log(double(5)); // Output: 10
```

Here, 'createMultiplier' is a higher-order function since it returns another function.

Finally, let's look at some common higher-order functions

in JavaScript and TypeScript:

1. **Array.map():** Applies a given function to each element of an array and creates a new array with the results.

```
const nums = [1, 2, 3, 4];
const doubledNums = nums.map((x: number) => x * 2);

console.log(doubledNums); // Output: [2, 4, 6, 8]
```

2. **Array.filter():** Filters an array based on a condition provided by a function.

```
const nums = [1, 2, 3, 4];
const evenNums = nums.filter((x: number) => x % 2 === 0);

console.log(evenNums); // Output: [2, 4]
```

3. **Array.reduce():** Reduces an array to a single value by executing a provided function on each element of the array.

```
const nums = [1, 2, 3, 4];
const sum = nums.reduce((accumulator: number, currentValue: number
    ) => accumulator + currentValue, 0);

console.log(sum); // Output: 10
```

In conclusion, higher-order functions are an essential concept in TypeScript and functional programming, and they are crucial for writing expressive, organic, and reusable code.

4.4   How can you create and use mixin classes in TypeScript?

In TypeScript, mixins are a pattern that allows you to create reusable pieces of code and combine them into classes. A mixin is a function that accepts a class and returns a new class with additional or modified functionality.

Let's look at an example of creating and using mixin classes in TypeScript.

Suppose we have two functionalities that we want to reuse in multiple classes: 'Loggable' and 'Serializable'. Here's how we can create mixin functions for these functionalities:

```
// Loggable mixin
type Constructor<T = {}> = new (...args: any[]) => T;

function Loggable<TBase extends Constructor>(Base: TBase) {
  return class extends Base {
    log() {
      console.log("Loggable mixin:", this);
    }
  };
}

// Serializable mixin
function Serializable<TBase extends Constructor>(Base: TBase) {
  return class extends Base {
    serialize() {
      return JSON.stringify(this);
    }
  };
}
```

Now, let's create a class 'Person' that uses these mixins:

```
class Person {
```

```
  constructor(public name: string, public age: number) {}
}

// Apply both mixins to Person class
const LoggableSerializablePerson = Serializable(Loggable(Person));

// Create a new instance and use mixin methods
const person = new LoggableSerializablePerson("Alice", 30);
person.log();
console.log(person.serialize());
```

Here, we defined mixin functions 'Loggable' and 'Serializable' by extending the provided 'Base' class and adding new methods. Then, we created a regular 'Person' class and combined it with these mixins using the 'Serializable(Loggable(Person))' syntax. This produces a new class that has all the functionalities of the 'Person', 'Loggable' and 'Serializable' mixins.

When creating a new 'LoggableSerializablePerson' instance, we can call both the 'log' and 'serialize' methods, as they have been mixed into the class.

In summary, creating and using mixin classes in TypeScript involves:

1. Define mixin functions that accept a base class and extend it with new functionality.

2. Apply mixins to a class by wrapping them around the class.

3. Create instances of the mixed class and use their mixed methods.

4.5   Can you explain how to create a 'declaration merging' in TypeScript?

In TypeScript, "declaration merging" is a process through which multiple declarations with the same name are combined into a single one. This allows you to augment existing types with new properties, merge module declarations, or even extend interfaces without explicitly extending them.

To demonstrate declaration merging, let's look at some examples:

1. Merging Interfaces:

When you have two or more interfaces with the same name, TypeScript automatically merges their properties into one interface.

```
interface Box {
    height: number;
    width: number;
}

interface Box {
    scale: number;
}

let newBox: Box = {
    height: 10,
    width: 10,
    scale: 2
};
```

Above, the two interfaces with the name 'Box' are merged, and the 'newBox' object can now use properties from both.

2. Merging Namespaces:

You can also merge namespaces with the same name.
When you do this, the exported members of each namespace are combined.

```
namespace Animals {
    export class Dog {
        bark() {
            console.log("Woof!");
        }
    }
}

namespace Animals {
    export class Cat {
        meow() {
            console.log("Meow!");
        }
    }
}

let myDog = new Animals.Dog();
let myCat = new Animals.Cat();
```

In the example above, the two 'Animals' namespaces are
merged, allowing you to use the 'Dog' and 'Cat' classes
under the 'Animals' namespace.

3. Merging Interfaces and Namespaces:

It is also possible to merge an interface declaration with
a namespace declaration that has the same name.

```
interface Greeting {
    message: string;
}

namespace Greeting {
    export function sayHello() {
```

```
        console.log('Hello');
    }
}
// Usage
let greeting: Greeting = {message: 'Hi there'};
Greeting.sayHello();
```

In this example, an interface 'Greeting' is merged with
a namespace 'Greeting'. The result is a single 'Greeting'
that has the property 'message' from the interface and the
'sayHello' function from the namespace.

Merging declarations simplify and extend existing types
or modules by combining their properties or members.
However, it is essential to use this feature judiciously,
since overusing it could lead to confusion and make code
harder to maintain.

4.6 How do you work with third-party type definitions, such as DefinitelyTyped, in TypeScript?

To work with third-party type definitions, such as DefinitelyTyped, in TypeScript, you will typically install the
corresponding type definition package using a package
manager like npm or yarn, and then import the appropriate types into your code. Here are the steps:

1. **Find the appropriate type definition package:** Search
for the corresponding type definition package on [Definite-

lyTyped repository](https://github.com/DefinitelyType-d/DefinitelyTyped) or on [npm](https://www.npmjs.com/). For example, if you're using the library 'lodash', the type definition package will usually be named '@types/lodash'.

2. **Install the type definition package:** Use a package manager like npm or yarn to install the type definition package. For example, to install the type definitions for 'lodash', use one of the following commands:

With npm:

```
npm install --save-dev @types/lodash
```

With yarn:

```
yarn add -D @types/lodash
```

3. **Import the necessary types from the installed package:** In your TypeScript code, you will need to import the types from the type definition package you just installed. For example, let's assume you have a TypeScript file called 'example.ts', where you want to use the 'merge' function from the 'lodash' library. You could import and use the types like this:

```
import { merge } from 'lodash';
const mergedObject = merge({ key1: 'value1' }, { key2: 'value2'
    });
```

4. **Using types from external packages in your own custom types:** You may need to define your own custom types that include properties or methods from the

external package. You can do this by extending or implementing the types from the external package. Here is an example using the 'Moment' type from the 'moment' library:

First, install the type definition package for 'moment':

```
npm install --save-dev @types/moment
```

Then, in your TypeScript code, you can extend or implement the imported types:

```
import { Moment } from 'moment';

// Extending the Moment type
class CustomMoment extends Moment {
  customMethod() { /*...*/ }
}

// Implementing the Moment interface
interface CustomMomentInterface extends Moment {
  customMethod(): void;
}
```

By following these steps, you can effectively work with third-party type definitions, such as DefinitelyTyped, in TypeScript to ensure proper type checking and autocompletion in your code.

4.7   Can you explain the difference between 'type' and 'interface' when defining a function type?

In TypeScript, both 'type' and 'interface' can be used to define a function type, but they have some differences in how they support features like declaration merging, readability, and the ability to extend or implement other types. Let's dive into these differences with examples.

1. Declaration Merging:

One significant difference between 'type' and 'interface' is that multiple interfaces with the same name automatically merge, while types with the same name will throw an error.

For example:

```
interface FooFn {
  (x: number): number;
}

interface FooFn {
  (y: string): string;
}

const foo: FooFn = (arg: number | string) => {
  // Dummy implementation
  return typeof arg === "number" ? arg * 2 : arg.toUpperCase();
};
```

Now, using 'type':

```
type FooFn = (x: number) => number;

type FooFn = (y: string) => string; // Error: Duplicate identifier
        'FooFn'.
```

2. Implementing and Extending:

Interfaces can 'extend' other interfaces, and classes can 'implement' them. This feature does not exist in 'type' directly, although you can use intersection types to achieve a similar purpose.

For example:

```
interface BaseFn {
  (x: number): number;
}

interface DerivedFn extends BaseFn {
  (x: number, y: number): number;
}

class MyFunction implements DerivedFn {
  // Implementation
}
```

Now, using 'type':

```
type BaseFn = (x: number) => number;

type DerivedFn = BaseFn & ((x: number, y: number) => number);

class MyFunction {
  // Implementation
}
```

3. Readability:

When defining a simple function type, using 'type' can be more concise and readable compared to 'interface'.

For example:

```
type SimpleFn = (x: number) => number;

interface SimpleFn {
  (x: number): number;
}
```

Both 'SimpleFn' definitions are equivalent, but the 'type' version is shorter and more straightforward.

In conclusion, if you need declaration merging, extending, or implementing other types, 'interface' is the way to go. However, if you want a simple function type and more concise syntax, 'type' can be a better choice.

4.8   What is a discriminated union in TypeScript and how can you use it?

A discriminated union (also known as a tagged union or disjoint union) is a powerful feature in TypeScript that allows you to combine multiple types into a single type. It helps in representing a set of distinct possible cases where each case has uniquely identifiable properties. The discriminated union is a special kind of union type where one of the properties is used as a tag or discriminator to determine the specific type.

To create and use discriminated unions in TypeScript, you

can follow these steps:

1. Define the types to be combined.

2. Add a common literal property (the tag) to differentiate each type.

3. Create a union type with the defined types.

4. Use type guards or switch-case statements to narrow down the specific type during runtime.

Let's look at an example. Suppose we're creating a graphics application with different shape objects like circles, rectangles, and triangles:

```typescript
// Step 1: Define the types to be combined
interface Circle {
  kind: 'circle';    // Step 2: Add a common literal property (the
        tag)
  radius: number;
}

interface Rectangle {
  kind: 'rectangle';
  width: number;
  height: number;
}

interface Triangle {
  kind: 'triangle';
  base: number;
  height: number;
}

// Step 3: Create a union type with the defined types
type Shape = Circle | Rectangle | Triangle;
```

Now, we can have a function to compute the area of any given shape:

```typescript
function getArea(shape: Shape): number {
  // Step 4: Use type guards or switch-case statements
  switch (shape.kind) {
    case 'circle':
```

```
      return Math.PI * shape.radius ** 2;
   case 'rectangle':
      return shape.width * shape.height;
   case 'triangle':
      return 0.5 * shape.base * shape.height;
   default:
      // Ensures exhaustiveness checking at compile-time
      const _exhaustiveCheck: never = shape;
      return _exhaustiveCheck;
   }
}
```

In this example, we first defined three types: 'Circle',
'Rectangle', and 'Triangle'. Then, added a common literal
property 'kind' with a different value for each type. Next,
we defined a discriminated union type 'Shape' using the
combination of these types. Finally, we used a switch-case
statement inside the 'getArea' function to narrow down
the specific type and computed the area of each shape
separately.

The discriminated union feature of TypeScript comes in
handy when you need to model and work with sets of
distinct possible cases in a type-safe manner.

4.9   Can you give an example of using a 'symbol' type in TypeScript?

In TypeScript, the 'symbol' type is used to create unique
identifiers. Symbols can be especially useful as object keys
to avoid name collisions when using third-party libraries.

Consider the following example:

```
// Create a unique symbol identifier:
const uniqueSymbol = Symbol("exampleSymbol");

// Use the symbol as a property key in an object:
const obj = {
  [uniqueSymbol]: "This␣is␣a␣unique␣value",
  someStringKey: "This␣is␣a␣regular␣string␣key␣value"
};

// Get the value associated with the symbol key:
console.log(obj[uniqueSymbol]); // Output: "This is a unique value
"
```

In this example, we create a unique symbol identifier called 'uniqueSymbol'. A description "exampleSymbol" is provided to the 'Symbol()' function, which is only used for debugging purposes and does not impact the uniqueness of the symbol.

Next, an object called 'obj' is created with two properties. The first property uses the unique symbol as its key, and the second property is a regular string key ('someStringKey').

Finally, we access and log the value associated with the 'uniqueSymbol' key in the 'obj'.

4.10   What is the 'keyof' operator in TypeScript and how can you use it?

The 'keyof' operator in TypeScript is a type operator that returns a union type of all the possible keys (strings, numbers, or symbols) that can be used to access properties of a given typed object. It's particularly useful when you want to create a function that can take an object and a key of that object, and TypeScript can enforce that the key provided exists on the object.

Here's an example of how you can use the 'keyof' operator:

Suppose you have a simple 'Person' interface:

```
interface Person {
  id: number;
  name: string;
  age: number;
}
```

Now, let's create a 'getProperty' function that returns the value of a key in a given object of type 'Person'.

```
function getProperty(person: Person, key: keyof Person): any {
  return person[key];
}
```

The 'key: keyof Person' parameter ensures that the 'key' argument passed to the 'getProperty' function is one of the valid keys of a 'Person' object (i.e., '"id"', '"name"', or '"age"').

This function implementation uses the 'keyof' operator to make sure that the passed key is a valid key for the given 'Person' object.

Here's an example of how the 'getProperty' function can be used:

```
const tom: Person = {
  id: 1,
  name: "Tom",
  age: 25,
};

console.log(getProperty(tom, "name")); // Output: "Tom"
console.log(getProperty(tom, "age")); // Output: 25

// This line would cause a TypeScript error: Argument of type '"
    invalid_key"' is not assignable to parameter of type 'keyof
    Person'.
//console.log(getProperty(tom, "invalid_key"));
```

Notice how the invalid key '"invalid_key"' would cause an error in TypeScript if it were not commented out. This is because the 'keyof' operator ensures that only valid keys can be used.

To summarize, the 'keyof' operator in TypeScript helps in creating type-safe code by enforcing that only valid keys are used to access properties of a given typed object.

4.11 How can you implement an abstract class in TypeScript?

In TypeScript, an abstract class is a class that cannot be instantiated directly, but can be used as a base class for other classes. Abstract classes can have abstract methods, which are declared without an implementation, and they must be implemented by derived classes. Abstract class is defined using the 'abstract' keyword.

Here's an example of how to implement an abstract class in TypeScript:

1. Create an abstract class:

```
abstract class Shape {
  protected x: number;
  protected y: number;

  constructor(x: number, y: number) {
    this.x = x;
    this.y = y;
  }

  abstract getArea(): number;
  abstract getPerimeter(): number;
}
```

In this example, we have an abstract class 'Shape' with two abstract methods, 'getArea()' and 'getPerimeter()'. The class also has a constructor that takes two arguments, 'x' and 'y'.

2. Define a derived class:

Now, let's define a class 'Rectangle' that derives from the abstract class 'Shape' and implements the required abstract methods:

```
class Rectangle extends Shape {
  private width: number;
  private height: number;

  constructor(x: number, y: number, width: number, height: number)
      {
    super(x, y);
```

```
    this.width = width;
    this.height = height;
}

// Implement the abstract methods from the base class
getArea(): number {
  return this.width * this.height;
}

getPerimeter(): number {
  return 2 * (this.width + this.height);
}
}
```

In this example, we extend the base class 'Shape', implement the required abstract methods 'getArea()' and 'getPerimeter()' and provide our own private properties ('width' and 'height') and constructor.

3. Instantiate the derived class and use the implemented methods:

Finally, we can create an object of the derived class 'Rectangle' and use its methods:

```
const myRectangle = new Rectangle(0, 0, 5, 8);
console.log(`Area: ${myRectangle.getArea()}`);
console.log(`Perimeter: ${myRectangle.getPerimeter()}`);
```

Here, we create a 'Rectangle' with 'x', 'y', 'width', and 'height' as '0', '0', '5', and '8', respectively. Then, we call the 'getArea()' and 'getPerimeter()' methods to calculate and print the area and perimeter of the rectangle.

In this way, abstract classes can be implemented in Type-Script.

4.12   Can you explain the concept of 'type narrowing' in TypeScript?

Type narrowing in TypeScript is the process of refining the type information of a variable based on checks or assertions performed in the runtime code. It helps the TypeScript compiler to further understand the type of a variable at a given point in the code, allowing more precise type checking and autocompletion for that variable.

Type narrowing can be achieved using various constructs in TypeScript, such as type guards, custom type guards, type predicates, discriminated unions, and 'as' or '¡ type assertions.

Let me explain with examples. Consider the following union type:

```
type Shape = Circle | Rectangle;
```

Now let's say we have a variable 'shape' of type 'Shape'. Initially, TypeScript only knows that 'shape' is either a 'Circle' or a 'Rectangle'.

```
const shape: Shape = getShape();
```

We can use type narrowing to further refine this type information, for example with a type guard using an 'if' statement.

```
if ("radius" in shape) {
    // Inside this block, TypeScript knows that 'shape' is of type
        'Circle'
} else {
    // Inside this block, TypeScript knows that 'shape' is of type
        'Rectangle'
}
```

Here's another example using discriminated unions. Suppose we have an 'Animal' type represented by a discriminated union of 'Dog' and 'Cat', differentiating them by the 'kind' property:

```
type Dog = {
    kind: "dog";
    bark: () => void;
};

type Cat = {
    kind: "cat";
    meow: () => void;
};

type Animal = Dog | Cat;
```

We can use type narrowing with a switch statement:

```
function handleAnimal(animal: Animal) {
    switch (animal.kind) {
        case "dog":
            // TypeScript knows 'animal' is of type 'Dog' in this
                case
            animal.bark();
            break;
        case "cat":
            // TypeScript knows 'animal' is of type 'Cat' in this
                case
            animal.meow();
            break;
    }
}
```

You can illustrate type narrowing with the following flowchart:

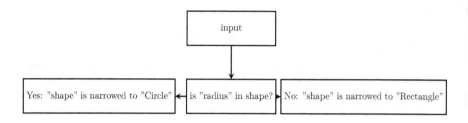

The code above can be represented like this:

$$\begin{cases} shape \xrightarrow{\text{"radius" in shape?}} \text{Yes} \implies \text{"shape" is narrowed to "Circle"} \\ shape \xrightarrow{\text{"radius" in shape?}} \text{No} \implies \text{"shape" is narrowed to "Rectangle"} \end{cases}$$

To summarize, type narrowing is the process of refining the type information of a variable in TypeScript, based on runtime checks or assertions. This allows the TypeScript compiler to provide more precise type checking and code suggestions for that variable.

4.13   What is 'strict mode' in Type-Script and what does it do?

Strict mode in TypeScript is a compiler option that enables a set of stricter type checking and safety features to help you write more robust, accurate, and maintainable code. It's represented by the '–strict' flag in the 'tsconfig.json' configuration file. When enabled, it activates several type checking and safety options, such as:

1. 'noImplicitAny' - Disallows any implicit 'any' types, forcing the programmer to provide type annotations.

2. 'noImplicitThis' - Disallows using 'this' in a function that's not inside a class or object when the type is not known.

3. 'alwaysStrict' - Enforces the use of 'use strict' directive; parses ECMAScript modules in strict mode.

4. 'strictNullChecks' - Disallows assigning 'null' or 'undefined' to non-nullable types.

5. 'strictFunctionTypes' - Tightens the type checking for functions, ensuring that they are of compatible types.

6. 'strictBindCallApply' - Ensures a more accurate type checking for 'bind', 'call', and 'apply' methods.

7. 'strictPropertyInitialization' - Ensures that class properties are initialized in the constructor, either directly or indirectly.

You can enable strict mode in the 'tsconfig.json' file like this:

```
{
  "compilerOptions": {
    "strict": true
  }
}
```

Here's an example to further illustrate the difference strict mode can make:

```
class Sample {
  name: string; // Without strict mode, this can be left
      uninitialized

  constructor(name?: string) {
    if (name) {
      this.name = name;
    }
```

```
  }

  printName() {
    console.log(this.name.toUpperCase());
  }
}

let instance = new Sample();
instance.printName(); // Throws a runtime error, since `name` is
    undefined
```

When strict mode is enabled, TypeScript will report an error on the 'name' property because it's not initialized. To fix this issue, you either need to provide a default value or declare it as a nullable type:

```
class Sample {
  name: string = "default"; // Provide a default value, or declare
    it as `string | undefined`

  constructor(name?: string) {
    if (name) {
      this.name = name;
    }
  }

  printName() {
    console.log(this.name.toUpperCase());
  }
}
```

In conclusion, strict mode helps you catch potential issues in your code during the development and compilation stages, thus ensuring your code is more robust and maintainable.

4.14 How do you use 'bigint' in TypeScript and what are its use cases?

In TypeScript, 'bigint' is a primitive data type that represents whole numbers larger than 253 - 1, which is the largest number that can be represented using the standard 'number' type in JavaScript. With 'bigint', you can store and perform arithmetic with very large integers.

To use 'bigint' in TypeScript, you can either:

1. Append the letter 'n' to the end of an integer literal, making it a 'bigint' literal, or

2. Use the 'BigInt' constructor function to convert a numerical string or another 'bigint' to a new 'bigint'.

Here's an example of using 'bigint' in TypeScript:

```
const maxSafeInteger: bigint = BigInt(Number.MAX_SAFE_INTEGER);
const one: bigint = BigInt(1);

const largeInteger: bigint = maxSafeInteger + one;
console.log(`Large Integer: ${largeInteger}`);
```

In this example, the 'Number.MAX_SAFE_INTEGER' constant is converted to a 'bigint' and stored in the 'maxSafeInteger' variable. We then define another 'bigint' variable 'one' with the value 1. Finally, we add 'maxSafeInteger' and 'one' together and store the result in 'largeInteger'.

When working with 'bigint', you should be aware that it

cannot be mixed with the 'number' type. For example,
you cannot directly add a 'bigint' to a 'number'. You will
need to convert the 'number' to 'bigint' before performing
any arithmetic.

```
const num: number = 42;
const bigNum: bigint = BigInt(num);

// This line will cause an error since you cannot mix bigint and
    number types
// const sum: bigint = num + bigNum;

// You must convert 'num' to a bigint before performing the
    addition
const sum: bigint = BigInt(num) + bigNum;
```

Regarding use cases for 'bigint', it can be useful in the
following scenarios:

1. **Cryptography**: 'bigint' can be used to handle large
integers when working with encryption, decryption, and key
generation algorithms.

2. **Arbitrary-precision mathematics**: For calculations
requiring high precision arithmetic, 'bigint' can provide accurate results.

3. **BigInt UUIDs**: Using 'bigint' instead of strings to
handle very large UUID values.

Overall, 'bigint' is especially useful when the size or precision requirements for integer values exceed the capabilities
of the standard 'number' type.

4.15 What are utility types in TypeScript and can you provide examples of their usage?

Utility types in TypeScript are a set of predefined generic types that help in various type manipulation tasks. They can be used to create new types based on existing types by modifying, picking, or omitting some parts of them. This powerful feature helps in making the code more maintainable, scalable, and robust by reusing existing types and keeping the type definitions DRY (Don't Repeat Yourself).

Here are some common utility types in TypeScript with their respective usage examples:

1. 'Partial<T>': Constructs a new type with all properties of 'T' set as optional.

```
interface Person {
  name: string;
  age: number;
}

type PartialPerson = Partial<Person>;

const person: PartialPerson = {
  name: 'John',
};
```

2. 'Readonly<T>': Constructs a new type with all properties of 'T' set as readonly.

```
interface Person {
  name: string;
  age: number;
```

```
}

type ReadonlyPerson = Readonly<Person>;

const person: ReadonlyPerson = {
  name: 'John',
  age: 30,
};

person.age = 31; // Error: Cannot assign to 'age' because it is a
    read-only property
```

3. 'Pick<T, K>': Constructs a new type by picking a set of properties 'K' from 'T'.

```
interface Person {
  name: string;
  age: number;
  email: string;
}

type PersonNameAndEmail = Pick<Person, 'name' | 'email'>;

const person: PersonNameAndEmail = {
  name: 'John',
  email: 'john@example.com',
};
```

4. 'Omit<T, K>': Constructs a new type by omitting a set of properties 'K' from 'T'.

```
interface Person {
  name: string;
  age: number;
  email: string;
}
type PersonWithoutEmail = Omit<Person, 'email'>;

const person: PersonWithoutEmail = {
  name: 'John',
  age: 30,
};
```

5. 'Record<K, T>': Constructs a new type with a set of property keys 'K' and corresponding value type 'T'.

```
type UserRole = Record<'admin' | 'user', string>;

const roles: UserRole = {
  admin: 'Administrator',
  user: 'Regular␣User',
};
```

6. 'Exclude<T, U>': Constructs a new type by excluding values from 'U' that are assignable to 'T'.

```
type T1 = Exclude<'a' | 'b' | 'c', 'a'>; // Result: 'b' | 'c'
```

7. 'Extract<T, U>': Constructs a new type by extracting values from 'U' that are assignable to 'T'.

```
type T1 = Extract<'a' | 'b' | 'c', 'a' | 'f'>; // Result: 'a'
```

8. 'NonNullable<T>': Constructs a new type by excluding 'null' and 'undefined' from 'T'.

```
type T1 = NonNullable<string | number | null | undefined>; //
    Result: string | number
```

These utility types can be combined and customized according to the requirements of your projects, making the type handling in TypeScript more flexible and powerful.

4.16   How can you use TypeScript to work with REST APIs?

TypeScript is a superset of JavaScript, which means it extends and improves its capabilities, making it an excellent choice for working with REST APIs. Here's a step-by-step guide on how to use TypeScript to work with REST APIs:

1. **Creating a TypeScript project**: First, set up a new TypeScript project by installing TypeScript globally.

```
npm install -g typescript
```

Create a new project folder and initialize it with 'npm init'.

```
mkdir ts-rest-api
cd ts-rest-api
npm init -y
```

Now, initialize the TypeScript project by running:

```
tsc --init
```

2. **Installing required libraries**: In this example, we will be using 'axios' to make HTTP requests and '@types/axios' for TypeScript definitions. To install these, run:

```
npm install axios
npm install --save-dev @types/axios
```

3. **Defining data types**: REST APIs deal with data, and it is crucial to define the data types and structure expected from the API response. For this example, let's assume the REST API returns a list of users with their 'id', 'name', 'email', and 'address'.

Create a new file named 'types.ts' and define the data types as follows:

```
export interface User {
    id: number;
    name: string;
    email: string;
    address: Address;
}

export interface Address {
    street: string;
    city: string;
    zipcode: string;
}
```

4. **Building a helper function to work with the REST API**: To make it easier to work with the REST API, you can create a helper function that abstracts the API calls. In this case, we will build a simple function that retrieves all users and another one to retrieve a specific user by ID.

Create a new file named 'api.ts', and implement the helper functions for fetching users:

```
import axios from 'axios';
import { User } from './types';

// Base URL for the REST API
const API_BASE_URL = 'https://jsonplaceholder.typicode.com';

export async function fetchUsers(): Promise<User[]> {
    const response = await axios.get<User[]>(`${API_BASE_URL}/users
        `);
    return response.data;
}

export async function fetchUserById(userId: number): Promise<User>
    {
    const response = await axios.get<User>(`${API_BASE_URL}/users/$
        {userId}`);
    return response.data;
}
```

5. **Using the helper functions**: Now that we defined the types and helper functions, we can use them to inter-

act with the REST API.

Create a new file named 'main.ts' and use the 'fetchUsers'
and 'fetchUserById' functions:

```
import { User } from "./types";
import { fetchUsers, fetchUserById } from "./api";

async function main() {
    const users: User[] = await fetchUsers();
    console.log("All users:");
    console.table(users);

    const singleUser: User = await fetchUserById(1);
    console.log("User with ID 1:");
    console.table(singleUser);
}

main();
```

6. **Compile and run the TypeScript code**: To compile
the TypeScript code to JavaScript, run:

```
tsc
```

This will generate a set of JavaScript files that can be
executed using Node.js. To run the 'main.js' file, execute:

```
node main.js
```

You will see the output with the list of all users and the
details of the User with ID 1 fetched from the REST API.

This example demonstrates a basic way of using Type-
Script to work with REST APIs. You can extend this
approach to perform other actions such as creating, updating, and deleting resources via the API using the 'axios' library and the defined data types.

4.17 Can you explain how 'this' works in TypeScript?

The 'this' keyword in TypeScript (and JavaScript) refers to the context in which a function is called. The value of 'this' is determined at runtime, when the function is invoked. In this explanation, we'll cover how 'this' works in different scenarios in TypeScript.

1. **Global context**: When a function is invoked outside of any class or object, 'this' refers to the global object ('window' in browsers, 'global' in Node.js). Here's an example:

```
function globalThisExample() {
  console.log(this);
}

globalThisExample(); // Output: Window (or global in a Node.js
    environment)
```

2. **Object context**: When a method is called on an object, 'this' refers to the object that the method is a property of.

```
class Animal {
  name: string;

  constructor(name: string) {
    this.name = name;
  }

  speak() {
    console.log(`Hello, my name is ${this.name}.`);
  }
}

const dog = new Animal('Buddy');
dog.speak(); // Output: Hello, my name is Buddy.
```

In the 'speak' method, 'this' refers to the 'dog' instance of the 'Animal' class.

3. **Class context**: In a class, 'this' refers to the instance of that class.

```
class Counter {
  private value: number = 0;

  increment() {
    this.value++;
    console.log(`Counter value: ${this.value}`);
  }
}
```

const myCounter = new Counter(); myCounter.increment(); // Output: Counter value: 1 "'

4. **Using 'bind', 'call', and 'apply'**: One can explicitly set the value of 'this' for a specific function using the 'bind', 'call', or 'apply' methods.

```
const person = { name: 'Alice' };

function greet() {
  console.log(`Hello, I'm ${this.name}.`);
}

const boundGreet = greet.bind(person);
boundGreet(); // Output: Hello, I'm Alice.

greet.call(person); // Output: Hello, I'm Alice.

greet.apply(person); // Output: Hello, I'm Alice.
```

5. **Arrow functions**: Arrow functions use lexical scoping for 'this', which means 'this' inside an arrow function is the same as its containing (outside) function.

```
class Timer {
  private timeout: number;
```

```
  constructor() {
    this.timeout = 1000;
  }

  start() {
    setTimeout(() => {
      console.log(`Timeout: ${this.timeout}ms`);
    }, this.timeout);
  }
}

const myTimer = new Timer();
myTimer.start(); // Output: Timeout: 1000ms
```

In the 'start' method, the arrow function retains the value of 'this' from the surrounding context (the instance of the 'Timer' class).

To sum up, the 'this' keyword in TypeScript refers to the context in which a function is called. This value depends on how the function is invoked, which can vary depending on whether it's called globally, on an object, using 'bind', 'call', or 'apply', or within an arrow function. Understanding these different contexts will help you effectively utilize the 'this' keyword in your TypeScript code.

4.18 What is 'type compatibility' in TypeScript and how does it work?

Type compatibility in TypeScript is a mechanism that determines whether two types can be considered "compatible" or assignable to each other. This feature allows Type-

Script to provide powerful type checking while maintaining flexibility in assigning values between different types. Type compatibility in TypeScript is based on structural typing, which means that it considers two types to be compatible if their structures (i.e., properties and methods) match, even if the names of the types are different.

To check if two types are compatible, TypeScript recursively compares the properties of these types, ensuring that the source type's properties have compatible properties in the target type. If each property in the source type can be found in the target type and their types are compatible, then the whole source type is considered compatible with the target type.

Let's go through some examples to better understand how type compatibility works in TypeScript:

1. Basic type compatibility:

```
interface Named {
  name: string;
}

class Person {
  name: string;
}

let p: Named;
// Here, Person and Named are compatible since both have a 'name'
    property of type string
p = new Person();
```

2. Function type compatibility:

```
interface Greet {
  (phrase: string): void;
}
```

```
function greet(g: Greet) {
  g("Hello,␣world!");
}

// Both of the following are compatible with the Greet interface.
const fn1 = (x: string) => console.log(x);
const fn2 = (x: string, y?: number) => console.log(x);

greet(fn1); // OK
greet(fn2); // OK
```

Function type compatibility is based on the function's parameter and return types. In the above example, both 'fn1' and 'fn2' are compatible with the 'Greet' interface since their parameter types and return types match.

3. Generic type compatibility:

```
interface Empty<T> {}

let x: Empty<number>;
let y: Empty<string>;

// Here, Empty<number> and Empty<string> are compatible since their
    structures (empty) are the same
x = y;
```

Generic types are compatible if their structures and type arguments are compatible. In the above example, both 'Empty<number>' and 'Empty<string>' have an empty structure, so they are considered compatible.

However, it's important to note that TypeScript's type compatibility is not always perfect, and there might be cases where it's too permissive or too strict. In such situations, you can use type assertions or custom type guards to fine-tune the type checking behavior.

Overall, type compatibility in TypeScript is a powerful

feature that allows flexible, yet robust type checking and makes it easier to work with different data structures and APIs while maintaining strong safety guarantees.

4.19   How do you configure a TypeScript project using 'tsconfig.json'?

To configure a TypeScript project using 'tsconfig.json', you need to follow these steps:

1. **Create a TypeScript project**: If you don't have a TypeScript project, create a new directory for your project and run 'npm init' to create a 'package.json' file. This will store metadata about your project and its dependencies. Install TypeScript via 'npm' by running the command 'npm install typescript –save-dev'.

2. **Create a tsconfig.json file**: In the root directory of your TypeScript project, create a new file named 'tsconfig.json'. This file is used to specify the options for compilation and other settings for your TypeScript project (such as the 'include' and 'exclude' array of file patterns).

3. **Configure the tsconfig.json file**: A minimal 'tsconfig.json' configuration might look like this:

```
{
  "compilerOptions": {
    "target": "es5",
```

```
    "module": "commonjs",
    "strict": true,
    "outDir": "./dist"
  },
  "include": ["src/**/*.ts"],
  "exclude": ["node_modules"]
}
```

This configuration specifies the following options:

- '"target": "es5"': This setting specifies the output JavaScript target version. Here it's set to ECMAScript 5 (ES5).

- '"module": "commonjs"': This setting defines the module system used in the output files. With "commonjs", the project will use the CommonJS module format.

- '"strict": true': This setting enables a wide range of type-checking behavior that results in stronger guarantees of program correctness. It is highly recommended for TypeScript projects.

- '"outDir": "./dist"': This setting specifies the output folder for the compiled JavaScript files. Here, the compiled files will be placed in the 'dist' folder.

- '"include": ["src/**/*.ts"]': This setting lists the file patterns to be included in the compilation process. In this example, all TypeScript files ('*.ts') in the 'src' folder and all its sub-folders will be included.

- '"exclude": ["node_modules"]': This setting lists the file patterns or folders to be excluded from the compilation process. Here, the 'node_modules' folder is excluded from the compilation process.

You can customize these options or add more options depending on your project requirements.

4. **Compile your TypeScript project**: To compile your TypeScript project, run the command 'tsc' (or 'npx tsc' if you have TypeScript installed as a local dependency) from the command line or terminal. TypeScript will read the 'tsconfig.json' file and compile your project using the specified options.

Here's a chart to visualize the compilation process configured by 'tsconfig.json':

In summary, to configure a TypeScript project using 'tsconfig.json', create a 'tsconfig.json' file in the project directory, mention the desired compiler options, include and exclude patterns, and run the TypeScript compiler using the 'tsc' command. This allows you to have full control over the compilation process and TypeScript's various options.

4.20   How can you handle module resolution in TypeScript?

In TypeScript, module resolution is the process of determining the location of a module's corresponding file at runtime. There are two strategies for module resolution in TypeScript: Classic and Node. The Node strategy is the default and recommended method for most use cases.

Before diving into module resolution strategies, it's essential to understand the difference between relative and non-relative imports.

Relative import paths (starting with '/', '../', or '/') explicitly indicate the location of the imported module relative to the importing module.

For example:

```
import { myFunction } from './myModule'; // Located in the same
    directory.
import { myFunction } from '../myModule'; // Located in the parent
    directory.
```

Non-relative import paths do not start with '/', '../', or '/'. They are typically resolved against the 'node_modules' directory, making them suitable for external library modules.

For example:

```
import { library } from 'someLibrary';
```

Now, let us discuss the two module resolution strategies:

1. **Classic Resolution Strategy:** This strategy mimics the behavior of the TypeScript compiler (version 1.0). For non-relative module imports, the compiler looks for a matching file (with a '.ts', '.tsx', '.d.ts', '.js', or '.jsx' extension) in the same directory as the importing module. If no match is found, the search moves up the directory tree until a file is found or the root is reached.

For relative module imports, the process is the same.
However, instead of starting in the same directory as the
importing module, the search starts at the relative path.

Classic resolution strategy could be set with 'tsconfig.json'
file:

```
{
  "compilerOptions": {
    "moduleResolution": "classic"
  }
}
```

2. **Node Resolution Strategy:** This strategy mimics
the module resolution behavior of the Node.js runtime.
For non-relative module imports, the compiler first looks
for a matching file in 'node_modules' directory, starting
in the same directory as the importing module. If no
match is found, the search moves up the directory tree
until a match is found or the root is reached. For relative
imports, the search starts at the relative path, just like in
the Classic strategy.

Node resolution strategy could be set with 'tsconfig.json'
file:

```
{
  "compilerOptions": {
    "moduleResolution": "node"
  }
}
```

It's important to note that when using Node resolution
with the "module" option set to "ES2015" or higher, Type-
Script follows the "Module Resolution" recommendation
from the ECMAScript standard. Therefore, it will resolve

imports according to the import map specified in the "imports" field of the 'package.json' file.

In conclusion, handling module resolution in TypeScript involves understanding the nature of your imports (relative or non-relative) and selecting the appropriate resolution strategy according to your project's requirements. The Node resolution strategy is generally preferred, as it aligns with the module resolution behavior of the Node.js runtime and is more familiar to developers coming from JavaScript.

Chapter 5

Expert

5.1 Can you describe how to set up and configure a build process for a TypeScript project?

Setting up and configuring a build process for a Type-Script project involves a few steps. The main components you will need are Node.js, the TypeScript compiler (tsc), and a build tool or task runner like npm scripts, Gulp, or Webpack. In this answer, I will cover how to use npm scripts with tsc to configure a build process.

1. **Install Node.js and npm**: First, make sure you have Node.js and npm (Node Package Manager) installed on your system. You can download Node.js from the of-

ficial website: https://nodejs.org/. npm comes bundled
with Node.js.

2. **Initialize the project**: From the terminal, navigate
to your project's root directory, and run the following
command to create a 'package.json' file:

```
npm init -y
```

3. **Install TypeScript locally**: To install the Type-
Script compiler locally in your project, run the following
command:

```
npm install --save-dev typescript
```

4. **Create a 'tsconfig.json' file**: This file contains the
TypeScript compiler options and is placed at the root of
your project. You can create one by running the following
command:

```
npx tsc --init
```

5. **Configure the 'tsconfig.json' file**: Open the 'tscon-
fig.json' file in your favorite text editor and set the desired
options. Here's an example configuration:

```
{
  "compilerOptions": {
    "target": "es2017",
    "module": "commonjs",
    "strict": true,
    "esModuleInterop": true,
    "sourceMap": true,
    "outDir": "dist"
  },
  "include": ["src/**/*.ts"],
  "exclude": ["node_modules", "**/*.spec.ts"]
}
```

In this configuration:

- The 'target' option specifies the output JavaScript version (here, ECMAScript 2017).

- The 'module' option defines the module system to use (here, commonJS).

- The 'strict' option enables strict type-checking.

- The 'esModuleInterop' option allows default imports from modules with no default export.

- The 'sourceMap' option generates source maps to enable debugging.

- The 'outDir' option defines the output directory for compiled JavaScript files (here, a 'dist' folder).

- The 'include' field specifies which TypeScript files should be compiled.

- The 'exclude' field specifies which files or directories should be ignored by the compiler.

6. **Add build scripts to 'package.json'**: Open your 'package.json' file and add the 'scripts' section. For example:

```
"scripts": {
  "prebuild": "rm -rf dist",
  "build": "tsc"
}
```

These scripts will:

- The 'prebuild' script removes the 'dist' folder if it exists to clear previous build outputs.

- The 'build' script compiles TypeScript files using the Type-Script compiler (tsc).

7. **Run the build process**: Now you can run the build process by executing the following command in your terminal:

```
npm run build
```

This will compile your TypeScript files according to the specified configuration and output the resulting JavaScript files in the 'dist' folder.

With these steps, you have successfully set up and configured a build process for your TypeScript project using npm scripts and tsc. Don't forget to add any additional packages, libraries, or build tools based on your project's requirements.

5.2   How can you use TypeScript with server-side frameworks like Express.js or NestJS?

TypeScript is a superset of JavaScript that allows you to write statically-typed code. It can be seamlessly integrated with server-side frameworks like Express.js or NestJS. In this answer, I will provide a detailed explanation of how to use TypeScript with these frameworks, including a basic setup and configuration.

1. Express.js with TypeScript:

To use TypeScript with Express.js, you need to follow these steps:

Step 1: Install the required packages:

You need to install 'typescript', '@types/express', '@types/node', and 'ts-node' as development dependencies. Run the following command to do so:

```
npm install --save-dev typescript @types/express @types/node ts-node
```

Step 2: Initialize a TypeScript project:

Create a 'tsconfig.json' file in your project's root folder and include the following configuration:

```
{
  "compilerOptions": {
    "target": "es6",
    "module": "commonjs",
    "outDir": "./built",
    "sourceMap": true,
    "esModuleInterop": true,
    "strict": true
  },
  "include": ["src/**/*.ts"],
  "exclude": ["node_modules"]
}
```

This configures TypeScript to compile your code into the './built' folder using the ES6 target and CommonJS module system.

Step 3: Write your Express.js application using TypeScript:

Create an 'src' folder in your project's root folder and create a 'server.ts' file inside it. Write your Express.js application using TypeScript:

```typescript
import express, { Request, Response } from 'express';

const app = express();
const port = 3000;

app.get('/', (req: Request, res: Response) => {
  res.send('Hello, TypeScript & Express!');
});

app.listen(port, () => {
  console.log(`Server is running on port ${port}`);
});
```

Step 4: Update your 'package.json' scripts:

Add the following scripts to your 'package.json':

```json
"scripts": {
  "start": "ts-node src/server.ts",
  "build": "tsc",
  "serve": "node built/server.js"
}
```

Now you can run the following commands:

- 'npm start': Run your TypeScript Express.js application directly.

- 'npm run build': Compile your TypeScript code into the './built' folder.

- 'npm run serve': Run the compiled JavaScript Express.js application from the './built' folder.

2. NestJS with TypeScript:

NestJS is a framework that's built with TypeScript by

default, so there isn't a separate setup process needed.
Just follow these steps:

Step 1: Install the NestJS CLI:

```
npm install -g @nestjs/cli
```

Step 2: Create a new NestJS project:

```
nest new project-name
```

Replace 'project-name' with your desired project name.

Step 3: Run the NestJS application:

Navigate to the newly created folder and run the following
command:

```
npm run start:dev
```

This will run your NestJS application in development
mode with TypeScript.

So, integrating TypeScript with server-side frameworks
like Express.js and NestJS is straightforward. It significantly improves code maintainability, enables autocompletion, and provides better error handling possibilities.

5.3   Can you explain the differences between 'as const' vs 'const' assertions in TypeScript?

In TypeScript, 'const' declarations and 'as const' assertions serve different purposes but are related in the sense that they both deal with immutability.

1. 'const' declarations:

'const' is used to declare a constant variable whose value cannot be changed after its initialization. It creates read-only references within the scope of the declaration.

```
const pi = 3.14159;
pi = 3.14; // TypeScript Error: Cannot assign to 'pi' because it is
    a constant or a read-only property.
```

2. 'as const' assertions:

'as const' assertion, introduced in TypeScript 3.4, is a way to make the entire structure (object or array) immutable, which means that once created, it cannot be modified. It also narrows the type of the literals used. This is commonly called "const assertions" or "const contexts."

For example, consider this code:

```
const colors = ['red', 'green', 'blue'] as const;

colors.push('yellow'); // TypeScript Error: Property 'push' does
    not exist on type 'readonly ["red", "green", "blue"]'.
```

When using the 'as const' assertion, TypeScript has inferred the 'colors' variable as an immutable tuple with the exact types of the strings ('"red"', '"green"', and '"blue"'), instead of the default mutable array of strings ('string[]').

Here's another example illustrating the differences between objects with and without 'as const':

```
const obj1 = {
  a: 1,
  b: 'hello',
};
// TypeScript infers 'obj1' as:
// {
//   a: number;
//   b: string;
// }

const obj2 = {
  a: 1,
  b: 'hello',
} as const;
// TypeScript infers 'obj2' as:
// {
//   readonly a: 1;
//   readonly b: "hello";
// }
```

To recap, here are the key differences between 'const' declarations and 'as const' assertions in TypeScript:

- 'const' is simply used to declare constant variables with an immutable value, while 'as const' is used for making an entire structure (object or array) read-only.

- 'const' declarations do not change the type of the variables, while 'as const' may narrow down the types of the variables (e.g., from 'number' to the specific value used in the literal).

In conclusion, 'const' is used to make variables read-only, while 'as const' is used to make an entire structure-of-

literals immutable and narrow down the types to their
exact literal values.

5.4   How do you handle transpilation of TypeScript into different versions of ECMAScript?

Handling the transpilation of TypeScript into different
versions of ECMAScript is done using the TypeScript
compiler (tsc) and configuring the appropriate options in
the 'tsconfig.json' file of your project.

In the 'tsconfig.json' file, you can specify the ECMAScript
version you want to transpile your TypeScript code into
by setting the "target" property. The "target" property
allows you to choose the desired ECMAScript version:
ES3, ES5, ES6/ES2015, ES2016, ES2017, ES2018, ES2019,
ES2020, ES2021, or ESNext. The default value for "target" is ES3.

To handle transpilation of TypeScript into different versions of ECMAScript, edit your 'tsconfig.json' file with the
corresponding target value. For example, if you want to
transpile your TypeScript code into ES2015 (also known
as ES6), update your 'tsconfig.json' to include:

```
{
  "compilerOptions": {
    "target": "ES2015"
  }
}
```

```
}
```

Let's say you have a simple TypeScript file 'example.ts':

```typescript
class MyClass {
  constructor(public name: string) {}

  greet() {
    return `Hello, ${this.name}!`;
  }
}

const instance = new MyClass("John");
console.log(instance.greet());
```

After transpiling to different ECMAScript versions using different "target" options in your 'tsconfig.json', you would observe the following differences in output:

1. '"target": "ES5"' (Classes will be transpiled to constructor functions with a prototype chain)

```javascript
var MyClass = (function () {
    function MyClass(name) {
        this.name = name;
    }
    MyClass.prototype.greet = function () {
        return "Hello, " + this.name + "!";
    };
    return MyClass;
}());
var instance = new MyClass("John");
console.log(instance.greet());
```

2. '"target": "ES2015"' (ES6 features, like classes, will be preserved)

```javascript
class MyClass {
    constructor(name) {
        this.name = name;
    }
    greet() {
        return `Hello, ${this.name}!`;
```

```
    }
}
const instance = new MyClass("John");
console.log(instance.greet());
```

Remember that targeting a higher ECMAScript version might result in a smaller output and better runtime performance, but it will require a more modern JavaScript runtime environment, which might not be supported in older browsers.

It's good practice to choose a transpilation target that balances compatibility with your project's requirements and the JavaScript environment where your code will run.

5.5   What is the concept of 'declaration files' in TypeScript and when should they be used?

In TypeScript, declaration files are used to provide type information about external libraries, modules or other code that is not written in TypeScript. They have the extension '.d.ts' and describe the public API of the code without providing an actual implementation. Declaration files are important because they allow you to leverage TypeScript's type checking and code editor intelligence features with external libraries or modules, making the development experience significantly better.

A declaration file typically contains interface and type definitions, as well as declarations for functions, classes, and variables. They can be written manually or generated using a tool such as 'dts-gen'.

Declaration files should be used when:

1. You want to use a JavaScript library in your TypeScript project: Declaration files provide TypeScript with information about the library's API, so you can utilize TypeScript's type checking and autocompletion features.

For instance, consider using the popular library 'lodash'. If you want to use it in your TypeScript project, you should install the corresponding declaration file:

```
npm install --save-dev @types/lodash
```

This will install the type definitions for 'lodash', allowing TypeScript to recognize the types and offer suggestions when using the library.

2. You are migrating a JavaScript project to TypeScript: Creating declaration files for the existing JavaScript code is a good starting point. It will help you catch type-related issues even before converting the entire codebase to TypeScript.

3. You are working with other projects or teams that use JavaScript: In such scenarios, it's a good practice to provide declaration files for better integration and collaboration with projects or developers that aren't using

TypeScript.

Here's an example of a simple declaration file:

```
// example.d.ts
declare module 'example' {
  interface Config {
    option1: string;
    option2: number;
  }

  function create(config: Config): void;

  const defaultConfig: Config;

  export { create, defaultConfig };
}
```

In this example, we are declaring a module 'example' with an 'interface Config', a 'function create', and a 'const defaultConfig'. The 'create' function takes a 'Config' object as an argument, and the 'defaultConfig' is exported as a 'const' of type 'Config'.

In summary, declaration files are essential when working with TypeScript to provide type checking, autocompletion, and other features that enhance the development process. They help in integrating external libraries, migrating JavaScript projects to TypeScript, and collaborating with JavaScript-oriented developers.

5.6 Can you explain how to use TypeScript with web workers?

Web Workers provide a way for running scripts in the background, without affecting the performance of the main page. They are especially useful when you need to perform CPU-intensive tasks without freezing the User Interface.

Here are the steps to use TypeScript with Web Workers:

1. **Create worker TypeScript file**: Start by creating a separate TypeScript file for the Web Worker. This file contains the code that will run in the background. Let's call it 'worker.ts':

```
self.addEventListener('message', (event: MessageEvent) => {
    const data = event.data;
    // Perform some expensive operation using data
    const result = data.map((x: number) => x * 2); // simple
        example
    (self as any).postMessage(result);
});
```

Here, we're listening to the 'message' event, which is triggered when the main thread sends a message to the worker. The worker then processes the data, and sends a message back to the main thread with the result.

2. **Compile worker TypeScript file**: In order to use this worker file in a web-browser, you need to compile it to JavaScript. For this purpose, create a 'tsconfig.worker.json' configuration file:

```
{
    "compilerOptions": {
        "target": "es5",
        "lib": ["webworker"],
        "module": "none",
        "outFile": "./worker.js"
    },
    "include": ["./worker.ts"]
}
```

Here, we tell TypeScript compiler to compile 'worker.ts'
file to 'worker.js' with target JavaScript version as 'es5'.
The 'lib' option is set to 'webworker', as we're working
with Web Workers.

Now, run the TypeScript compiler:

```
tsc --project ./tsconfig.worker.json
```

This will generate a 'worker.js' file in the specified folder.

3. **Create main TypeScript file**: Next, create the
main TypeScript file, e.g., 'main.ts', to communicate with
the Web Worker:

```
if (window.Worker) {
    const worker = new Worker('worker.js');

    worker.onmessage = (event: MessageEvent) => {
        const result = event.data;
        console.log('Result from worker:', result);
    };

    worker.onerror = (event: ErrorEvent) => {
        console.error('Error from worker:', event.message);
    };

    const dataToSend = [1, 2, 3, 4, 5];
    worker.postMessage(dataToSend);
} else {
    console.error('Web Workers are not supported in your browser.')
        ;
}
```

Here, we first check if the browser supports Web Workers. If supported, we create a new instance of the Worker with 'worker.js', set up the 'onmessage' and 'onerror' event listeners and send a message to the worker using its 'postMessage' method.

4. **Compile main TypeScript file**: Compile the main TypeScript file by adding the required configurations to your 'tsconfig.json' or creating a new configuration file, e.g., 'tsconfig.main.json'.

In this example, I'll create a new configuration file:

```
{
    "compilerOptions": {
        "target": "es5",
        "lib": ["dom", "esnext"],
        "module": "none",
        "outFile": "./main.js"
    },
    "include": ["./main.ts"]
}
```

Now, run the TypeScript compiler:

```
tsc --project ./tsconfig.main.json
```

5. **Connect the compiled script to your HTML**: Finally, include 'main.js' in your HTML file:

```
<!DOCTYPE html>
<html lang="en">
  <head>
    <meta charset="UTF-8" />
    <meta name="viewport" content="width=device-width,␣initial-
        scale=1.0" />
    <title>TypeScript and Web Workers</title>
  </head>
  <body>
    <script src="main.js"></script>
  </body>
```

```
</html>
```

That's it! Now you know how to use TypeScript with
Web Workers. You can use this setup as a base to create
and utilize Web Workers for more complex operations.

5.7   What are some strategies for migrating a large JavaScript codebase to TypeScript?

Migrating a large JavaScript codebase to TypeScript can
be a complex and time-consuming task, but it's worth the
effort as TypeScript brings static typing, better tooling
support, and improved code maintainability. Here are
some strategies to make the process more manageable:

1. **Incremental migration:** Break down the migration process into smaller parts by converting individual
JavaScript files into TypeScript gradually. This ensures
your codebase remains functional at all times during the
transition, and the impact of the change is limited to specific parts of the codebase.

2. **Choose a strict configuration:** Consider using strict
mode in your 'tsconfig.json' file to enable strictest Type-
Script compiler options, ensuring the highest level of type
safety. However, note that strict mode can be challenging to implement in large projects, so you may need to

balance strictness with practicality.

3. **Refactor and modularize the codebase:** Before converting the code, identify and resolve any fundamental issues, such as tightly-coupled modules, and refactor the code to make it more modular and maintainable. This not only makes the conversion to TypeScript easier, but also results in an overall cleaner codebase.

4. **Make use of type annotations and interfaces:** TypeScript allows you to define custom types, interfaces, and type annotations, which can be used to provide type information for existing JavaScript code. This can help the TypeScript compiler to better understand your code, and find potential issues during the migration process.

5. **Use JSDoc comments:** For parts of the code that remain in JavaScript, you can use JSDoc comments to provide type information. TypeScript can infer types from these comments, allowing you to gain some benefits of TypeScript's type checking without converting the entire file.

6. **Leverage third-party type definitions:** When using third-party libraries, leverage type definitions provided by the open-source community through DefinitelyTyped or similar resources. These provide interfaces and type annotations for popular libraries, making it easier to integrate them into your TypeScript project.

7. **Understand and address errors reported by the TypeScript compiler:** The TypeScript compiler is your pri-

mary tool for identifying and fixing type-related issues.
Be prepared to spend time addressing reported errors and
working through them methodically for best results.

8. **Refactor post-migration code:** Once a JavaScript
file has been converted to TypeScript, take the opportu-
nity to refactor the new TypeScript code to use TypeScript-
specific features like generics, enums, and advanced type
manipulation. This helps ensure that you get the most
value from your migration.

9. **Test and validate the code:** Throughout the migration process, ensure that your tests remain up-to-date,
and continuously validate your code. This helps you catch
potential issues early in the migration process and ensures
that the final TypeScript code is functionally equivalent
to the original JavaScript.

10. **Learn from your team's experiences:** As your
team becomes more familiar with TypeScript, encourage
team members to share their learnings, best practices, and
lessons learned from the migration, so the team as a whole
benefits from the collective wisdom.

In summary, migrating a large JavaScript codebase to
TypeScript requires a methodical approach, dividing the
process into manageable steps, and consistently refining
and validating the code throughout the process. By using
the strategies outlined above, you'll increase your chances
of a successful migration, ultimately benefiting from the
advantages TypeScript has to offer.

5.8   Can you provide an example of using 'type predicates' in TypeScript?

Type predicates are very useful in TypeScript when you want to assert that a specific value belongs to a specific type within a function, and create a hint to TypeScript about that. A type predicate has the form 'parameter-Name is Type'.

Let's imagine a simple example. Suppose we have these two classes:

```
class Circle {
  constructor(public radius: number) {}
}

class Square {
  constructor(public sideLength: number) {}
```

Now suppose that we want to create a function that takes a shape (either a 'Circle' or a 'Square') and tests if it is a 'Circle'. We can use a type predicate for that:

```
function isCircle(shape: Circle | Square): shape is Circle {
  return (shape as Circle).radius !== undefined;
}
```

In the function above, we checked if the property 'radius' exists in the 'shape' object. If it exists, we know that it's a 'Circle'. The 'shape is Circle' part of the function signature is the type predicate, implying if the function returns 'true', TypeScript will know that the shape is a

'Circle'.

Here's an example of using our 'isCircle' function:

```
const circle = new Circle(5);
const square = new Square(4);

if (isCircle(circle)) {
  console.log("It's a circle with radius", circle.radius); //
      TypeScript knows circle is a Circle.
} else {
  console.log("It's a square with side length", circle.sideLength)
      ; // TypeScript knows circle is a Square.
}

if (isCircle(square)) {
  console.log("It's a circle with radius", square.radius); //
      TypeScript knows square is a Circle.
} else {
  console.log("It's a square with side length", square.sideLength)
      ; // TypeScript knows square is a Square.
}
```

In the example above, when we use 'isCircle(circle)', Type-Script knows that if 'isCircle' returns 'true', then 'circle' must actually be an instance of 'Circle'. Similarly, when 'isCircle(square)' returns 'false', it knows that 'square' is an instance of 'Square'.

5.9   How would you use TypeScript with a GraphQL API?

To use TypeScript with a GraphQL API, you would typically follow these steps:

1. Set up your TypeScript environment.

2. Install necessary dependencies for GraphQL and set up a GraphQL client.

3. Generate TypeScript types for your GraphQL schema.

4. Write TypeScript types for your GraphQL queries, mutations, and subscriptions.

5. Use your GraphQL client to execute these operations in your TypeScript application.

Let's break down each step in detail.

1. Set up your TypeScript environment

First, you need to set up a TypeScript project. You can follow the official TypeScript guide for initial setup: [TypeScript in 5 minutes](https://www.typescriptlang.org/docs/handbook/typescript-in-5-minutes.html)

2. Install GraphQL dependencies and set up GraphQL client

To interact with a GraphQL API, you will need a GraphQL client. Two popular choices are Apollo Client and URQL. In this example, we will use the Apollo Client. First, install the necessary dependencies:

```
npm install @apollo/client graphql
```

Now, set up an instance of Apollo Client in your Type-Script project. Let's assume you have 'API_URL' as your GraphQL endpoint.

```
import { ApolloClient, InMemoryCache } from '@apollo/client';

export const client = new ApolloClient({
  uri: 'API_URL',
  cache: new InMemoryCache(),
});
```

3. Generate TypeScript types for your GraphQL schema

For a better developer experience and type safety, you should generate TypeScript types based on your GraphQL schema. You can use the [GraphQL Code Generator](https://graphql-code-generator.com/) for this purpose.

First, install the necessary dependencies:

```
npm install -D @graphql-codegen/cli @graphql-codegen/typescript
    @graphql-codegen/typescript-operations
```

Then, create a 'codegen.yml' configuration file in your project root directory with the following content:

```
overwrite: true
schema: 'API_URL'
documents: 'src/**/*.graphql'
generates:
  src/generated/graphql.ts:
    plugins:
      - 'typescript'
      - 'typescript-operations'
```

Replace ''API_URL'' with your actual GraphQL endpoint. Now, run the following command to generate types for your GraphQL schema:

```
npx graphql-codegen
```

4. Write TypeScript types for your GraphQL queries, mutations, and subscriptions

Now, you can define your GraphQL operations using Type-Script. First, create a '.graphql' file to write your queries, mutations, or subscriptions. For example, create a file named 'userData.graphql' with this content:

```graphql
query GetUser($id: ID!) {
  user(id: $id) {
    id
    name
    email
  }
}
```

After running the GraphQL Code Generator ('npx graphql-codegen'), you will have TypeScript types for your 'GetUser' query inside 'src/generated/graphql.ts'.

5. Use your GraphQL client to execute operations in your TypeScript application

Now you can use the Apollo Client to execute the 'GetUser' query in your TypeScript application:

```typescript
import { client } from './apolloClient';
import { useQuery } from '@apollo/client';
import { GetUser, GetUserVariables } from './generated/graphql';
import getUserQuery from './userData.graphql';

// Usage in a React component, for example.
const UserComponent = (props: { id: string }) => {
  const { data, loading, error } = useQuery<GetUser,
      GetUserVariables>(getUserQuery, {
    variables: { id: props.id },
  });

  if (loading) return <div>Loading...</div>;
  if (error) return <div>Error: {error.message}</div>;

  return (
    <div>
      <h1>Name: {data?.user?.name}</h1>
      <h2>Email: {data?.user?.email}</h2>
    </div>
  );
```

```
};
```

In this example, we used the 'useQuery' hook from Apollo Client to fetch the user data with their ID, and then rendered the data using a React component.

By following these steps, you can create a typed, type-safe environment when working with a GraphQL API in a TypeScript project.

5.10   Can you explain the difference between 'nominal typing' and 'structural typing' and how TypeScript relates to these concepts?

Nominal typing and structural typing are two different ways programming languages handle type comparisons and assignments. They differ in the way they handle type compatibility between objects and classes/interfaces. Here are their definitions and how TypeScript relates to these concepts:

1. Nominal Typing:

In languages that use nominal typing, two types are considered compatible if they have the same declared type.

That is, two objects are considered to have the same type
if they were explicitly derived from the same class, interface, or provided type label. Nominal typing is also called
name-based typing because it compares types based on
their names.

Here's an example in a hypothetical smooth pseudo-code
that uses nominal typing:

```
class Person {
    name: string;
}

class Employee {
    name: string;
}

const person: Person = new Person();
const employee: Employee = new Employee();

// This would result in a type error, even though both objects
      share
// the same properties and structure.
person = employee;
```

In this example, even though the 'Person' and 'Employee'
classes have the same structure, they are considered to be
different types because they have been explicitly labeled
as such.

2. Structural Typing:

Languages that use structural typing consider two types
compatible if they have the same structure—i.e., if an
object has all the properties that another object requires,
the two objects are considered to have the same type.
Structural typing is also called "duck typing" or "shape-
driven typing."

TypeScript is a **structurally-typed** language, meaning
that it uses structural typing to determine type compatibility.

Here's an example of the same 'Person' and 'Employee'
classes in TypeScript:

```
interface Person {
    name: string;
}

interface Employee {
    name: string;
}

const person: Person = { name: "Alice" };
const employee: Employee = { name: "Bob" };

// This is okay in TypeScript because both templates share
// the same structure.
person = employee;
```

In this TypeScript example, the 'person' and 'employee'
objects can be assigned to each other because their structures match, even though they are annotated with different interface names.

In summary, TypeScript is a structurally-typed language,
which means it checks the compatibility between types
based on their structures, rather than their names. This
behavior allows for more flexibility in code organization
and enables better code reuse without having to explicitly
extend or implement common interfaces.

5.11 How can you create a custom decorator in TypeScript?

Creating a custom decorator in TypeScript involves defining a function with a specific signature that TypeScript recognizes as a decorator. Decorators can be applied to classes, class properties, methods, accessors, and method parameters. In this explanation, I will provide detailed steps to create a custom class decorator, method decorator, and property decorator.

Let's start with a class decorator. A class decorator is a function that takes a constructor as its argument and returns either void or a new constructor (if you want to replace the class):

```
function ClassDecorator<T extends { new(...args: any[]): {} }>(
    constructor: T) {
    // Perform operations on the constructor, e.g., add or modify
        methods.
    return class extends constructor {
        // Add or override properties or methods.
    };
}
```

Usage example:

```
@ClassDecorator
class MyClass {
    constructor(public name: string) {}
}

const myInstance = new MyClass("John␣Doe");
```

Next, let's create a custom method decorator. A method decorator is a function that takes three arguments: target

(the prototype of the class), propertyKey (method name),
and descriptor (property descriptor), and returns a new
descriptor or void:

```
function MethodDecorator(target: Object, propertyKey: string |
    symbol, descriptor: PropertyDescriptor): PropertyDescriptor |
    void {
  // Perform operations on the descriptor or the target, e.g.,
      modify the method implementation.
}
```

Usage example:

```
class AnotherClass {
  @MethodDecorator
  sayHello(name: string): string {
    return `Hello, ${name}!`;
  }
}
```

Lastly, let's create a custom property decorator. A property decorator is a function that takes two arguments:
target (the prototype of the class) and propertyKey (property name), and returns nothing:

```
function PropertyDecorator(target: Object, propertyKey: string |
    symbol): void {
  // Perform operations on the target or create/modify metadata.
}
```

Usage example:

```
class ThirdClass {
  @PropertyDecorator
  public greeting: string;

  constructor(greeting: string) {
    this.greeting = greeting;
  }
}
```

That's it! Now you know how to create custom decorators in TypeScript for classes, methods, and properties. Just make sure that you have enabled the "experimentalDecorators" option in your 'tsconfig.json' file:

```
{
  "compilerOptions": {
    "experimentalDecorators": true
  }
}
```

5.12 How do you optimize TypeScript compilation time for larger projects?

Optimizing TypeScript compilation time for larger projects can significantly improve the developer experience and increase productivity. Here are some best practices and techniques to achieve this.

1. **Use 'tsconfig.json' options:**

Configuring the 'tsconfig.json' file allows you to optimize TypeScript compilation. Some useful options include:

a) '"incremental": true': This setting enables TypeScript's incremental compilation, which caches the results of compilation for faster subsequent builds.

b) '"skipLibCheck": true': By skipping type checking for declaration files ('*.d.ts'), you can reduce the compilation time.

c) '"isolatedModules": true': Enabling isolated modules forces each file to be treated as a separate module. This option can improve build times in scenarios with many files and a large dependency graph.

Here's a sample 'tsconfig.json':

```
{
  "compilerOptions": {
    "incremental": true,
    "skipLibCheck": true,
    "isolatedModules": true,
    "target": "es5",
    "module": "commonjs"
  }
}
```

2. **Use '–transpileOnly' flag:**

The '–transpileOnly' flag skips the type checking step during TypeScript compilation. This option is preferable for development or when type checking is done separately. For example, with 'ts-loader', you can set the 'transpileOnly' option to 'true':

```
{
  test: /.tsx?$/,
  use: 'ts-loader',
  options: {
    transpileOnly: true,
  },
  exclude: /node_modules/,
}
```

3. **Leverage 'project references':**

For very large projects or monorepos, you can use Type-

Script's project references feature. It allows you to break your project into smaller, more manageable parts with separate 'tsconfig.json' files. By specifying references, you can ensure that builds only recompile the affected segments of the dependency tree.

Here's a sample project structure:

```
root/
  tsconfig.json
  packages/
    package-a/
      tsconfig.json
      src/
    package-b/
      tsconfig.json
      src/
```

In each 'tsconfig.json' of 'package-a' and 'package-b', you can set the 'composite' option:

```
{
  "compilerOptions": {
    "composite": true,
    // other options
  },
  // ...
}
```

In the root 'tsconfig.json', you specify the references:

```
{
  "references": [
    { "path": "./packages/package-a" },
    { "path": "./packages/package-b" },
  ]
}
```

4. **Parallelize Build Process:**

When using 'ts-loader' or other loaders with webpack, you

can also parallelize the type checking process with the 'HappyPack' or 'thread-loader' packages.

For example, using 'thread-loader' in combination with 'ts-loader':

```
{
  test: /.tsx?$/,
  use: [
    { loader: 'thread-loader' },
    { loader: 'ts-loader' },
  ],
  exclude: /node_modules/,
}
```

By applying these best practices and techniques, you can significantly optimize the TypeScript compilation time for larger projects.

5.13   What are some ways to handle interoperability between TypeScript and JavaScript in a codebase?

Handling interoperability between TypeScript and JavaScript in a codebase can be achieved through various methods. Here we will be discussing some of the commonly used approaches:

1. **Gradual Integration:**

Gradually integrating TypeScript into a JavaScript code-base is an effective strategy. Start by converting the most critical or complex parts of the application to TypeScript, and then progressively move on to the other parts.

To do this, rename the '.js' files that you wish to convert to '.ts'. TypeScript will generate the respective '.js' output files after you compile the TypeScript code. You should use the 'allowJs' compiler option in your 'tsconfig.json' file:

```
{
  "compilerOptions": {
    "allowJs": true,
  }
}
```

2. **Declaration Files:**

Use TypeScript declaration files ('.d.ts') for third-party JavaScript libraries or for some parts of your JavaScript codebase that you do not wish to convert right away. These declaration files provide TypeScript with the necessary information about types, interfaces, and functions, without you having to rewrite your entire codebase.

For example, if you have the following JavaScript function:

```
// helper.js
function add(a, b) {
  return a + b;
}
```

You can create a corresponding declaration file:

```
// helper.d.ts
declare function add(a: number, b: number): number;
```

3. **Typed Superset:**

With TypeScript being a typed superset of JavaScript, it means that all valid JavaScript code is also valid TypeScript code. By treating all '.js' files as TypeScript (using the 'allowJs' option mentioned in method 1), you can make use of TypeScript's type inference capabilities. This approach will allow TypeScript to gradually infer types within your project, without requiring manual type annotations.

4. **Comments for Type Information (JSDoc):**

TypeScript also allows you to provide type information within JavaScript files using JSDoc comments. This way, you do not have to convert your JavaScript files to TypeScript just to utilize TypeScript's type-checking abilities. Here's an example:

```
/**
 * @param {number} a
 * @param {number} b
 * @return {number}
 */
function add(a, b) {
  return a + b;
}
```

5. **JavaScript Versus TypeScript Interoperability:**

Whenever you need to interact between TypeScript and JavaScript, you can use type assertions (casting) to make sure that the data you receive from the JavaScript side is properly typed within your TypeScript code. For example, if you have a JavaScript function named 'getDatabase-DataAsJson', which returns JSON data, you can assert its type in TypeScript like below:

```
interface DatabaseData {
  id: number;
  name: string;
}

const jsonData: string = getDatabaseDataAsJson();
const databaseData: DatabaseData = JSON.parse(jsonData) as
    DatabaseData;
```

In summary, handling interoperability between TypeScript and JavaScript in a codebase can be achieved through gradual integration, declaration files, typed superset, JS-Doc comments, and type assertions. The choice of method(s) to use depends on your specific requirements, project size, and team knowledge.

5.14   Can you explain how to use mapped types with conditional types in TypeScript?

Mapped types and conditional types are powerful features in TypeScript that allow us to create new, complex types based on existing ones. Let's briefly define each concept before diving into examples on how to use them together.

Mapped Types allow us to create new types by trans-

forming the properties of an existing type. They use a
'for...in' clause to iterate through each property in the
original type.

Conditional types are a way to express type relationships that depend on the relationship between types
themselves. They allow you to create types based on conditions, using the syntax 'T extends U ? X : Y'.

Now, let's see an example of how to use mapped types
with conditional types:

```
type MappedConditional<T> = {
    [K in keyof T]: T[K] extends (infer U)[] ? U : T[K];
};
```

The 'MappedConditional' type takes an object type 'T'
as its generic parameter, iterates through each property,
and checks if the property's value ('T[K]') is an array. If
so, it maps the array element's type ('U') as the output
type, else it maps the original type 'T[K]'.

Consider the following example:

```
type ExampleType = {
    anArray: number[];
    stringWithValue: string;
    nestedArray: string[][];
};

type TransformedExampleType = MappedConditional<ExampleType>;
```

'TransformedExampleType' would be equivalent to the
following type:

```
type TransformedExampleType = {
    anArray: number;
```

```
    stringWithValue: string;
    nestedArray: string[];
};
```

Here's another example to understand better how conditional types work within the mapped type:

```
type ExtractedReturnType<T> = T extends (...args: any[]) => infer
    R ? R : never;

type MappedReturnTypes<T> = {
    [K in keyof T]: ExtractedReturnType<T[K]>;
};

function foo(): number {
    return 42;
}

function bar(): string {
    return 'hello';
}

type FunctionsType = {
    fooFunction: typeof foo;
    barFunction: typeof bar;
};

type ReturnTypes = MappedReturnTypes<FunctionsType>;
```

In this example, we first create a utility type 'ExtractedReturnType'. This type takes 'T' as its generic parameter, checks if 'T' is a function, and gets the return type of the function ('R') using the 'infer' keyword. If 'T' is not a function, it resolves to 'never'.

Then, we create the mapped type 'MappedReturnTypes' that goes over each property in the generic 'T' and maps them to their respective return types using the 'ExtractedReturnType' utility type.

In our example, 'MappedReturnTypes<FunctionsType>' creates a new type 'ReturnTypes' that contains the return types of the function properties:

```
type ReturnTypes = {
    fooFunction: number;
    barFunction: string;
};
```

In summary, using mapped types with conditional types in TypeScript enables you to create new, complex types based on the properties and structure of existing types. These powerful features help ensure type safety and code maintainability when working with a variety of data structures and functions.

5.15   What are some common performance issues you can encounter when using TypeScript and how can you mitigate them?

There are several performance issues that can arise when using TypeScript. Some of the common performance issues and their mitigation strategies are:

1. **Long compilation times**

TypeScript adds a compilation step to the development process, which can lead to long build times in some cases, especially when dealing with large codebases or complex projects.

Mitigation strategies:

- Use the '–incremental' flag when compiling, which saves dependency information and only recompiles files that have changed.

- Use 'ts-loader' or 'awesome-typescript-loader' for faster bundling in Webpack builds.

2. **Slow type checking**

Type checking large codebases with many dependencies and complex types can sometimes cause slow type checking.

Mitigation strategies:

- Use '–skipLibCheck' flag to skip type checking of declaration files ('*.d.ts') during compilation.

- Refactor complex type definitions into simpler, easier-to-check types.

- Avoid overly complex or large union and intersection types.

- Limit the depth and complexity of mapped and conditional types.

3. **Large output file sizes**

TypeScript can generate large output files when transpiling your code, potentially affecting the performance of your application at runtime.

Mitigation strategies:

- Use bundling tools like Webpack or Rollup to minify and tree-shake the generated JavaScript code.

- Use the '–importHelpers' flag to move helper functions into a single imported file instead of duplicating them across output files.

4. **Memory usage**

TypeScript compiler can consume significant amounts of memory when compiling large projects or dealing with large type definitions.

Mitigation strategies:

- Use the '–maxNodeModuleJsDepth' flag to limit the depth of node module import tracing.

- Use the '–jsxFactory' option to specify a custom JSX factory, reducing the amount of memory consumed while transpiling JSX syntax.

Below are two examples illustrating the usage of flags:

Example of tsconfig.json using '–incremental' and '–skipLibCheck' flags:

```
{
  "compilerOptions": {
    "incremental": true,
    "skipLibCheck": true,
    // Other options...
  }
}
```

Example of a Webpack configuration using 'ts-loader':

```
const path = require('path');
module.exports = {
  mode: 'production',
  entry: './src/main.ts',
  output: {
    path: path.resolve(__dirname, 'dist'),
    filename: 'main.bundle.js',
  },
  resolve: {
    extensions: ['.ts', '.tsx', '.js', '.jsx'],
  },
  module: {
    rules: [
      {
        test: /.tsx?$/,
        use: 'ts-loader',
        exclude: /node_modules/,
      },
    ],
  },
};
```

In conclusion, TypeScript is a powerful language that delivers many benefits, but we need to be mindful of the potential performance issues that it can introduce. By employing the mitigation strategies mentioned above, you can optimize your development workflow and the runtime performance of your TypeScript applications.

5.16   Can you explain the concept of 'type widening' and 'type narrowing' in TypeScript?

In TypeScript, the process of determining specific types/values for variables during the code analysis is known as "type narrowing" and "type widening". Let's discuss each concept in more detail.

Type Widening:

Type widening occurs when TypeScript tries to infer a
more general type for a variable or expression that doesn't
have a specific type annotation. This is done to provide
more flexibility with the types when dealing with values
that might come from different sources, allowing Type-
Script to avoid errors due to a narrower type being inferred.

Example:

```
let myVar = "hello"; // myVar is inferred as type 'string',
                     // even though its value is "hello"
```

In the example above, TypeScript infers the type of 'my-
Var' as 'string' instead of the specific literal type '"hello"'
(which is more narrow). This is an example of type widening.

Type Narrowing:

Type narrowing refers to the process of refining the type
of a variable based on conditions or checks which make
TypeScript more confident about the specific type of the
variable. By using type guards or type predicates, you can
help TypeScript know a more specific type for a variable,
narrowing its type and providing better type checking.

Example:

```
function isString(value: any): value is string {
```

```
    return typeof value === "string";
}

function doSomethingWith(value: string | number): void {
  if (isString(value)) {
    // In this block, TypeScript knows 'value' is of type 'string'
    const length = value.length;
  } else {
    // In this block, TypeScript knows 'value' is of type 'number'
    const square = value * value;
  }
}
```

In the example above, we have a 'doSomethingWith' function that takes a value of type 'string | number'. The type guard 'isString' narrows the type of 'value' to 'string' when the condition is true, and consequently narrows the type of 'value' to 'number' when the condition is false.

To summarize, type widening relates to inferring a more general type for variables without specific type annotations, while type narrowing involves refining the type using type guards, predicates, or conditions that help TypeScript determine a more specific type.

5.17   How would you use TypeScript with a package manager like npm or yarn?

When you want to use TypeScript with a package manager like 'npm' or 'yarn', you would generally follow these steps:

1. Install Node.js and a package manager (npm or yarn).

2. Initialize the project and generate 'package.json'.

3. Install TypeScript and other required dependencies.

4. Configure TypeScript by creating a 'tsconfig.json' file.

5. Write TypeScript code and compile it.

6. Use external TypeScript packages and type definitions.

Now, let's go through these steps in greater detail:

1. Install Node.js and a package manager (npm or yarn)

First, install Node.js from the official website: https://nodejs.org/

'npm' is bundled with Node.js, while 'yarn' can be installed separately with the following command:

```
npm install -g yarn
```

2. Initialize the project and generate 'package.json'

Create a new project directory and navigate to it in the terminal. Initialize the project using package manager to generate 'package.json' file:

For 'npm':

```
npm init
```

For 'yarn':

```
yarn init
```

Follow the prompts to set up your project configuration.

3. Install TypeScript and other required dependencies

Install TypeScript as a development dependency using your package manager:

For 'npm':

```
npm install --save-dev typescript
```

For 'yarn':

```
yarn add --dev typescript
```

Additionally, install any other required dependencies for your project.

4. Configure TypeScript by creating a 'tsconfig.json' file

Create a 'tsconfig.json' file in your project root, to configure TypeScript compiler options. Here is a basic example of a 'tsconfig.json':

```
{
  "compilerOptions": {
    "target": "es5",
    "module": "commonjs",
    "strict": true,
    "outDir": "./dist",
    "sourceMap": true
  },
  "include": ["./src/**/*.ts"],
```

```
  "exclude": ["node_modules"]
}
```

This configuration tells TypeScript to compile '.ts' files in the 'src/' directory, output the compiled JavaScript files to the 'dist/' directory, and use strict type-checking.

5. Write TypeScript code and compile it

Create a 'src/' directory to write your TypeScript code in. For example, create a 'src/index.ts' file with the following content:

```
function greet(name: string): void {
  console.log(`Hello, ${name}!`);
}

greet("TypeScript");
```

Add a script to your 'package.json' to compile TypeScript:

```
"scripts": {
  "build": "tsc"
}
```

Compile your code by running 'npm run build' or 'yarn build', and the compiled JavaScript will be output to the 'dist/' directory.

6. Use external TypeScript packages and type definitions

To use external TypeScript packages, you need to install the package and its corresponding type definitions (if available). Type definitions are usually available under the '@types/' namespace.

For example, if you want to use the 'lodash' library, you would do:

For 'npm':

```
npm install lodash
npm install --save-dev @types/lodash
```

For 'yarn': "'bash yarn add lodash yarn add –dev @types/lodash "'

Then, you can import and use the 'lodash' library in your TypeScript code:

```
import _ from 'lodash';

const exampleArray = [1, 2, 3, 4, 5, 6];

const shuffledArray = _.shuffle(exampleArray);

console.log(shuffledArray);
```

That's it! You've now set up a TypeScript project with a package manager (npm or yarn), allowing you to manage dependencies and use external packages.

5.18   How do you use 'symbol' and 'bigint' in advanced TypeScript scenarios?

In advanced TypeScript scenarios, the use of 'symbol' and 'bigint' can be beneficial for various cases. These two data

types were introduced to handle specific problem domains
that were not well-covered by existing data types.

'symbol' is a unique and immutable data type introduced
to enable unique keys in objects, especially for avoiding
name clashes among properties in complex code. Whenever you create a new symbol, it's guaranteed to be unique,
and it can never be changed.

'bigint' is the newest numeric data type in TypeScript
designed to provide support for arbitrarily large integers
natively. Previously, integer values were represented using the 'number' type, which could only handle integer
values up to '2**53 - 1' (i.e., 'Number.MAX_SAFE_IN-
TEGER').

Let's go through examples that show the advanced usage
of 'symbol' and 'bigint' in TypeScript.

Advanced Usage of 'symbol'

1. Defining unique property keys in objects or classes:

```typescript
const firstName = Symbol("firstName");
const lastName = Symbol("lastName");

class Person {
  [firstName]: string;
  [lastName]: string;

  constructor(first: string, last: string) {
    this[firstName] = first;
    this[lastName] = last;
  }

  getFullName(): string {
    return this[firstName] + "␣" + this[lastName];
  }
}
```

```
const p = new Person("John", "Doe");
console.log(p.getFullName()); // "John Doe"
```

2. Defining constants with non-overlapping values (similar to enumerated types):

```
const Red = Symbol("Red");
const Green = Symbol("Green");
const Blue = Symbol("Blue");

type Color = typeof Red | typeof Green | typeof Blue;

function getColorName(color: Color): string {
  switch (color) {
    case Red:
      return "Red";
    case Green:
      return "Green";
    case Blue:
      return "Blue";
  }
}

console.log(getColorName(Green)); // "Green"
```

Advanced Usage of 'bigint'

1. Performing arithmetic on large integers:

```
const largeNumber: bigint =
    12345678901234567890123456789012345678901234567890n;
const anotherLargeNumber: bigint =
    98765432109876543210987654321098765432109876543210n;

const sum: bigint = largeNumber + anotherLargeNumber;
const product: bigint = largeNumber * anotherLargeNumber;

console.log(`Sum: ${sum}`);
console.log(`Product: ${product}`);
```

2. Handling large file sizes or other large quantities:

```
type FileSizeBytes = bigint;

class File {
  name: string;
```

```
  size: FileSizeBytes;

  constructor(name: string, size: FileSizeBytes) {
    this.name = name;
    this.size = size;
  }

  getSizeInGigabytes(): string {
    const bytesInGigabyte: bigint = 1_024n * 1_024n * 1_024n;
    const gigabytes: bigint = this.size / bytesInGigabyte;
    return `${gigabytes} GB`;
  }
}

const largeFile = new File("example.txt", 50n * 1_024n * 1_024n *
    1_024n);
console.log(largeFile.getSizeInGigabytes()); // "50 GB"
```

These examples should give you a good idea of some advanced scenarios where 'symbol' and 'bigint' can help you create more robust and reliable TypeScript code.

5.19   Can you explain how to write unit tests for TypeScript code?

Writing unit tests for TypeScript code is a crucial step for ensuring that your code works correctly and is free from bugs. This will also help with maintainability and collaboration. The most popular testing frameworks used in TypeScript projects are Jest and Mocha, along with assertion libraries like Chai.

In this answer, I will explain how to write unit tests for TypeScript code using Jest, which is the most popular choice.

First, you need to set up your TypeScript project for testing with Jest.

1. **Install necessary dependencies:**

```
npm install --save-dev jest @types/jest ts-jest typescript
```

You can also use 'yarn' to install the packages if you prefer:

```
yarn add --dev jest @types/jest ts-jest typescript
```

2. **Create a Jest configuration file:**

Create a new file in the root of your project called 'jest.config.js' and copy the following content:

```
module.exports = {
  preset: 'ts-jest',
  testEnvironment: 'node',
};
```

3. **Update package.json:**

Add the following scripts for running tests and generating coverage reports in your 'package.json' file:

```
"scripts": {
  "test": "jest",
  "test:coverage": "jest --coverage",
  ...
}
```

4. **Write your tests:**

Now, let's write a simple TypeScript function and a corresponding unit test.

File: 'add.ts' (The function to be tested)

```
export function add(a: number, b: number): number {
  return a + b;
}
```

File: 'add.test.ts' (The unit test file)

```
import { add } from './add';

describe('add', () => {
  test('it should add two numbers correctly', () => {
    const result = add(3, 4);
    expect(result).toBe(7);
  });

  test('it should handle negative numbers', () => {
    const result = add(-2, 5);
    expect(result).toBe(3);
  });
});
```

In the test file, we import the 'add' function, and then we use 'describe' and 'test' functions from Jest to organize and define our test cases. Inside each test case, we use 'expect' along with a Jest matcher (e.g., 'toBe', 'toEqual', 'toBeFalsy', etc.) to make assertions on the behavior of the 'add' function.

5. **Run the tests:**

To run the tests, use the following command:

```
npm test
```

If everything is set up correctly, you should see output indicating that the tests passed.

Here's a chart illustrating the testing process using Jest:

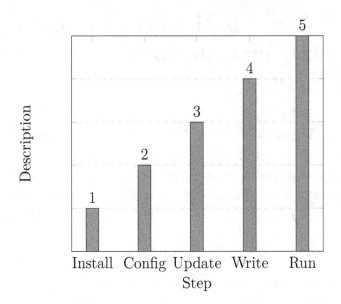

In summary, to write unit tests for TypeScript code, you can follow these steps:

1. Install necessary dependencies for testing (e.g., Jest, Type-Script, and other TypeScript type definitions).

2. Configure your TypeScript project for testing with Jest.

3. Update your 'package.json' to include test scripts.

4. Write your TypeScript tests using 'describe', 'test', and 'expect' functions from Jest.

5. Run the tests using the 'npm test' command.

By following these steps, you can ensure the correctness and quality of your TypeScript code and make your code maintainable and collaborative.

5.20   What is the process of set-ting up a monorepo with Type-Script?

Setting up a monorepo with TypeScript involves several steps, including initializing your monorepo project, con-figuring your workspaces, and setting up TypeScript and other dependencies. I'll go into each of these steps in de-tail.

1. **Initialize your monorepo project**

Begin by creating a new directory for your monorepo and initializing a new package using 'npm' or 'yarn'.

```
mkdir my-monorepo
cd my-monorepo
npm init -y
```

Or with 'yarn':

```
yarn init
```

2. **Configure Yarn or NPM workspaces**

Workspaces are a feature provided by package managers like Yarn and NPM to manage monorepos by linking all your packages together.

For Yarn, open your 'package.json' file and add the fol-lowing:

```
{
```

```
  "name": "my-monorepo",
  "private": true,
  "workspaces": [
    "packages/*"
  ]
}
```

For NPM, open your 'package.json' file and add the following:

```
{
  "name": "my-monorepo",
  "private": true,
  "workspaces": [
    "packages/*"
  ]
}
```

Create a directory called 'packages' in the root of your monorepo.

```
mkdir packages
```

3. **Add TypeScript and other dependencies**

Next, add TypeScript, '@types/node', and 'ts-node' as dev dependencies.

```
npm i --save-dev typescript @types/node ts-node
```

Or with 'yarn':

```
yarn add -D typescript @types/node ts-node
```

4. **Create and configure tsconfig.json**

In the root of your monorepo, create a 'tsconfig.json' file, which will contain the shared TypeScript configuration for all packages.

```
{
  "compilerOptions": {
    "target": "ES5",
    "module": "commonjs",
    "strict": true,
    "esModuleInterop": true,
    "moduleResolution": "node",
    "resolveJsonModule": true,
    "skipLibCheck": true,
    "forceConsistentCasingInFileNames": true,
    "outDir": "dist",
    "declaration": true,
    "baseUrl": ".",
    "paths": {
      "*": [
        "node_modules/*",
        "packages/*/*/src"
      ]
    }
  },
  "include": [
    "packages/**/*"
  ],
  "exclude": [
    "node_modules",
    "packages/**/node_modules"
  ]
}
```

5. **Create your first package**

Then, create a new package within the 'packages' directory.

```
mkdir packages/my-first-package
cd packages/my-first-package
npm init -y
```

Or with 'yarn':

```
yarn init
```

In 'packages/my-first-package/package.json', set the 'main',
'typings', and add a 'build' script like so:

```
{
  "name": "my-first-package",
  "version": "1.0.0",
  "main": "dist/index.js",
  "typings": "dist/index.d.ts",
  "scripts": {
    "build": "tsc␣--build"
  }
}
```

Now, create a 'src' folder within 'packages/my-first-package'
and add an 'index.ts' file.

6. **Create a reference in tsconfig.json**

In the root 'tsconfig.json', add a reference to your package:

```
{
  "references": [
    { "path": "packages/my-first-package" }
  ]
}
```

Repeat steps 5 and 6 for each additional package you want
to add to your monorepo.

7. **Build and use your packages**

Now you can run the 'build' script of your individual packages with:

```
npm run build
```

Or with 'yarn':

```
yarn build
```

Your individual packages can then import and use other

packages within your monorepo like any other external package.

With these steps, you have successfully set up a monorepo using TypeScript. As your project grows, you can easily add new packages and manage your interdependencies within your monorepo, improving the reusability and maintainability of your code.

Chapter 6

Guru

6.1 Can you describe some architectural patterns for structuring large-scale TypeScript applications?

It's important to have a well-structured architecture when working with large-scale TypeScript applications to facilitate maintainability, scalability, and testability. Here are some popular architectural patterns for structuring large-scale TypeScript applications:

1. **Layered architecture**

In a layered architecture, the application is divided into separate layers, where each layer has a specific responsibility and communicates with other adjacent layers. One such configuration is the 'Three-Tier Architecture' comprising three layers:

- Presentation Layer: Deals with the user interface and user experience.

- Business Logic Layer: Contains the business logic and domain-specific rules.

- Data Access Layer: Manages interactions with databases or other data storage systems.

Layering makes the code modular and easy to maintain. Here's a sample directory structure for this architecture:

```
src
    presentation
        components
        views
    business
        services
        models
    data
        repositories
        entities
    tests
```

2. **Domain-Driven Design (DDD)**

Domain-Driven Design (DDD) is a software development approach that focuses on the core domain and its logic. It encourages dividing the application into modular, domain-focused components known as 'Bounded Contexts'. Each Bounded Context represents a specific area of the business/domain and defines its own models, services, and repositories.

An important concept in DDD is the 'Aggregate', which is a group of related entities that should be treated as a single unit. The main entity in the aggregate is called the 'Aggregate Root'.

This architecture can be effective for large applications with complex and varied business logic. A sample directory structure for DDD could look like this:

```
src
    contexts
        context1
            aggregates
            services
            repositories
        context2
            aggregates
            services
            repositories
    tests
```

3. **Model-View-Controller (MVC)**

Model-View-Controller (MVC) is a design pattern for building user-facing applications. In TypeScript applications, specifically frontend applications, MV* patterns like Model-View-ViewModel (MVVM), and Model-View-Presenter (MVP) can also be effective. In MVC, the application is divided into:

- Model: Represents the domain data and business logic.

- View: Renders the domain data and captures user actions.

- Controller: Handles user input, manipulates the model, and updates the view accordingly.

Typical directory structure for an MVC architecture could
be:

```
src
   models
   views
   controllers
tests
```

For MV* patterns in a frontend architecture using framework like Angular, you might see:

```
src
   app
      components
      services
      models
tests
```

Each of these architectural patterns has its own advantages and disadvantages. It's essential to choose the one
that best fits the specific requirements and goals of the
project. In practice, these patterns can also be combined
or adapted to create a custom architecture tailored to the
project's needs.

6.2   How can you leverage Type-Script's type system to enforce specific architectural constraints?

Leveraging TypeScript's type system to enforce specific
architectural constraints can provide several benefits, such
as ensuring code consistency, improving maintainability,

and reducing the likelihood of defects. To achieve this, you can use the following concepts and features:

1. **Type Aliases**: Create custom types for architectural components, making it easier to understand their purpose and enforce specific constraints.

```
type UserID = string;
type UserName = string;

// Use custom types
function getUser(id: UserID): UserName {
    // ...
}
```

2. **Interfaces**: Define the structure of complex objects or components, ensuring they adhere to specific architectural patterns.

```
// Interface for a typical data repository
interface Repository<T> {
    getById(id: number): T | null;
    getAll(): Array<T>;
    save(entity: T): void;
}
```

3. **Abstract Classes**: Enforce specific contracts or behavior by using abstract classes as base classes for architectural components.

```
abstract class BaseController<T> {
    protected abstract repository: Repository<T>;

    getById(id: number): T | null {
        return this.repository.getById(id);
    }

    getAll(): Array<T> {
        return this.repository.getAll();
    }
}
```

4. **Namespaces**: Group architectural components or utility functions into separate namespaces, providing better organization and avoiding name conflicts.

```
namespace Validation {
    export interface Validator<T> {
        isValid(value: T): boolean;
    }

    export class EmailValidator implements Validator<string> {
        isValid(email: string): boolean {
            // Perform email validation logic
        }
    }
}
```

5. **Mapped Types**: Create new types by mapping through existing ones, changing properties or modifiers in the process.

```
type ReadOnly<T> = { readonly [K in keyof T]: T[K] };

// Example Usage
interface User {
    id: number;
    name: string;
}

type ReadOnlyUser = ReadOnly<User>;
```

6. **Conditional Types**: Apply specific constraints based on the input type, showing their utility in complex architectures.

```
type JSONValue =
    | string
    | number
    | boolean
    | null
    | JSONArray
    | JSONObject;
type JSONified<T> = {
    [K in keyof T]: T[K] extends JSONValue
        ? T[K]
        : T[K] extends Array<any>
```

```
      ? JSONifiedArray<T[K]>
      : JSONifiedObject<T[K]>
};

type JSONArray = Array<JSONified<any>>;
type JSONObject = JSONifiedObject<any>;
interface JSONifiedObject<T> {
  [P in keyof T]: (T[P] extends object) ? JSONified<T[P]> : T[P];
}
```

In summary, leveraging TypeScript's powerful type system can help you enforce and maintain specific architectural constraints throughout your codebase. By using a combination of type aliases, interfaces, abstract classes, namespaces, mapped types, and conditional types, you can create code that adheres to the desired architectural patterns, ensuring consistency and maintainability.

6.3 What's your approach to managing and evolving shared types in a large TypeScript codebase?

Managing and evolving shared types in a large TypeScript codebase can be challenging, but a systematic approach can help keep the code clean and maintainable. Here are some steps to achieve this:

1. **Organize Types in Shared Modules**

Create a separate directory for shared types, e.g., 'src/-types' or 'src/shared'. Organize your types in properly-named modules that can be easily imported and used across your codebase.

For instance, if you have shared types related to user management:

```
src/
  types/
    user.ts
```

And inside 'user.ts':

```
export interface User {
  id: number;
  name: string;
  email: string;
}

export type UserRole = 'admin' | 'user';
```

2. **Leverage Namespace**

Use TypeScript namespaces to group related types and interfaces. This can help in organizing your shared types and make managing large codebases easier.

```
namespace MyTypes {
  export interface User {
    id: number;
    name: string;
    email: string;
  }

  export type UserRole = 'admin' | 'user';
}
```

3. **Prefer Composition**

For complex types that share similar properties, use composition to avoid code duplication.

Example:

```
interface Timestamps {
  createdAt: Date;
  updatedAt: Date;
}

export interface User extends Timestamps {
  id: number;
  name: string;
  email: string;
}
```

4. **Refactor and Iterate Types**

As your codebase grows and evolves, it's essential to continuously refactor and iterate shared types. This includes updating types to make them more performant, eliminating duplicated or outdated types, and improving the maintainability of the code.

5. **Semantic Versioning and Type Changes**

When updating shared types in a library, follow semantic versioning best practices. This includes incrementing the major version number whenever breaking changes are introduced to the shared types, which notifies the users of the library that they need to take action to accommodate those changes.

6. **Use Code Reviews and Pull Requests**

Encourage team members to create pull requests for any changes made to the shared types. This allows the team to review the changes, discuss their implications, and establish consensus on how to handle type updates.

7. **Write Unit Tests**

Unit tests are crucial for detecting regressions in shared
types. Ensure that your shared types are well-covered by
tests, so when there's a change, you quickly identify any
issues.

8. **Create Documentation**

Write clear and concise documentation for your shared
types, explaining their purpose and usage. This helps
other developers understand the logic behind the design
and usage of your shared types.

9. **Use Type Aliases and Mapped Types**

Type aliases allow you to create new names for existing types, making the code more expressive and easier to
maintain. Mapped types can help you create new types
based on the transformations of existing types, reducing
code repetition.

Example:

```
type UserId = number;

interface ReadOnlyUser {
  readonly id: UserId;
  readonly name: string;
  readonly email: string;
}
```

10. **Auto-generate TypeScript Definition files**

If your codebase includes several packages or libraries, it
might be beneficial to auto-generate TypeScript definition
files ('*.d.ts') using tools like the TypeScript compiler.

This allows you to distribute types and interfaces via npm, making it easier for users to work with the library's API.

By following these steps, you will be able to manage and evolve shared TypeScript types effectively in a large codebase, ensuring better code quality and maintainability.

6.4　How do you handle versioning of TypeScript declaration files in a large project?

Handling versioning of TypeScript declaration files in a large project requires careful planning and organization. Here, I'll outline some best practices and strategies you can use to manage your TypeScript declaration files effectively.

1. **Organize your files with namespaces and modules**: It's important to structure your files in a way that's easy to manage as your project grows. Organize the declaration files of your project into separate namespaces (if applicable) or into separate files for each module.

```
// math.ts
export namespace Math {
  export function add(x: number, y: number): number;
  export function subtract(x: number, y: number): number;
}
```

2. **Use version control systems**: Use a version control

system (such as Git) to manage your project's source code, including your TypeScript declaration files ('*.d.ts'). This allows you to keep track of every change, revert to previous versions, and branch your codebase for different releases.

3. **Semantic versioning**: Adopt a semantic versioning (SemVer) scheme for managing the versions of your project. SemVer relies on three identifiers ('MAJOR.MINOR.PATCH'). Breaking changes require incrementing the 'MAJOR' version, while adding new features or improving the codebase without breaking backward compatibility bumps up the 'MINOR' version. Bug fixes and small, non-breaking changes increment the 'PATCH' version. Following SemVer principles ensures that developers using your library are not caught off-guard by breaking changes.

4. **Include version information in the declaration file**: One way to inform users of the current version is to include the version information directly within the declaration file. An example of this is as follows:

```
declare namespace MyLibrary {
  // Other definitions
  const version: string;
}
```

5. **Publish different versions to NPM or a private repository**: If your project is a reusable library, it's useful to publish the different versions of your TypeScript declaration files (and corresponding JavaScript code) to a package repository like NPM. This way, other developers can

reference specific library versions via package.json.

6. **Keep separate branches for different major versions**:
If you need to support multiple major versions of your
project simultaneously, create separate branches in your
version control system (e.g., Git) for each major version.
This way, you can still make fixes and improvements to
older versions while working on the main branch for the
next major release.

```
master (main development branch, targeting next release)
  |
  1.x (branch for maintaining version 1.x)
  |
  2.x (branch for maintaining version 2.x)
```

7. **Use 'typeVersions' field in package.json**: If your
TypeScript library has versions with different type declarations for different TypeScript versions, you can use the
'typesVersions' field in your package.json to specify which
declaration files should be used for different TS versions.
This is particularly useful when introducing types that
are only available in the newer TypeScript versions.

```
{
  "name": "my-library",
  "version": "1.0.0",
  "types": "index.d.ts",
  "typesVersions": {
    ">=3.1": {
      "*": ["ts3.1/*"]
    }
  }
}
```

In summary, managing TypeScript declaration files' versioning in a large project requires careful organization
and planning. By following these best practices like se-

mantic versioning, organizing your code using modules
and namespaces, leveraging version control systems, and
utilizing branches and the 'typesVersions' field in pack-
age.json, you'll make your TypeScript project easier to
maintain and keep track of changes over time.

6.5 How would you handle collision of namespaces in TypeScript at scale?

Handling namespace collisions in TypeScript at scale can
be a challenge, but it can be managed through the use
of well-designed coding practices and TypeScript features
like modules. Here are some strategies you can use to
handle namespace collisions:

1. **Use modules**: TypeScript modules are the preferred method of organizing and encapsulating the code
at scale. They inherently avoid namespace collisions by
keeping all their code within a local scope that doesn't
pollute the global namespace. A module can export and
import specific elements to manage visibility between different logical code separations:

```
// moduleA.ts
export function foo() {
}


// moduleB.ts
import { foo } from './moduleA';
```

```
foo();
```

2. **Prefix custom namespaces**: If you really need to use namespaces, it's a good practice to prefix custom namespaces with a unique identifier (e.g., company or project name) that is less likely to cause a collision:

```
namespace MyCompany_MyProject_MyNamespace {
  export function foo() {
  }
}
```

3. **Merge and augment namespaces**: TypeScript provides a feature called namespace merging, this allows you to split the contents of a namespace across multiple files while having the original namespace recognize the additions.

```
// file1.ts
namespace MyNamespace {
    export function foo() {}
}


// file2.ts
namespace MyNamespace {
    export function bar() {}
}
```

When the generated JavaScript code from above TypeScript is used, both functions 'foo' and 'bar' are available on the 'MyNamespace' object.

4. **Avoid polluting the global namespace**: Whenever possible, avoid placing your code directly in the global namespace. This will reduce the risk of collisions and make your code more modular and portable.

```
// Avoid this
function someGlobalFunction() {
}
```

5. **Use aliases**: If you are consuming external libraries
and suspect potential namespace conflicts, you can import
namespaces using aliases.

```
namespace ExternalLibNamespace {
    export function doSomething() {}
}
namespace MyAppNamespace {
    import doSomethingFunc = ExternalLibNamespace.doSomething;
    export function main() {
        doSomethingFunc();
    }
}
```

In conclusion, to handle namespace collisions in Type-
Script at scale, consider using modern TypeScript modules, which provide better encapsulation and reduce the
risk of collisions. If you must use namespaces, ensure
you follow best practices like prefixing namespaces, merging and augmenting namespaces when needed, avoiding
polluting the global namespace, and using aliases when
consuming external libraries.

6.6 What considerations would you keep in mind while building a library to be consumed by other TypeScript projects?

When building a library to be consumed by other Type-Script projects, several considerations should be taken into account to ensure a smooth and easy integration. Here are some of the key factors to consider:

1. **Type Definitions**: One of the main benefits of using TypeScript is the type safety it provides, so it's essential to export type definitions for your library. You should include a declaration file ('.d.ts') or make sure TypeScript generates one during the build process. This will allow users of your library to benefit from autocompletion, type checking, and other TypeScript features.

```
// example.d.ts
export interface ExampleInterface {
    foo: string;
    bar(): number;
}
```

2. **Documentation**: Document the library's public API, types, and methods thoroughly. This will help users understand how to use your library and ensure its smooth integration into their projects. Consider using JSDoc or TSDoc to annotate your code and generate documentation automatically.

```
/**
```

```
 * An example function that takes a number and returns the
     double of the number.
 * @param num - The number to double
 * @returns The double of the provided number
 */
export function exampleFunction(num: number): number {
    return num * 2;
}
```

3. **Tree Shaking**: Optimize your library for tree shaking to reduce the final bundle size for users. This can be done by exporting small, focused functions or classes that can be easily eliminated by bundlers like Webpack or Rollup if they are not used. Use ES modules instead of CommonJS modules for better tree shaking support.

4. **Polyfills and External Dependencies**: Minimize the use of polyfills and external dependencies to reduce bundle size and potential conflicts. Clearly document any required polyfills or dependencies, along with any peer dependencies that are expected to be provided by the consuming project.

5. **Extensibility and Customization**: Design your library API with extensibility and customization in mind. This can include exposing hooks, events, or even higher-order components to ensure your library is flexible and can adapt to various requirements of the consuming project.

6. **Modular Structure**: Organize your library in a modular structure, separating concerns and allowing users to import only what they need. This can help with tree shaking and bundle size optimization.

```
// src/index.ts
export { default as componentA } from './componentA';
```

```
export { default as componentB } from './componentB';
  ...
```

7. **Versioning**: Use semantic versioning ('semver')
to manage your library's releases. This will allow users
to understand the changes introduced in each version and
ensure they are using a compatible version of your library.

8. **Testing**: Write unit, integration, and end-to-end
tests to ensure your library's functionality and compatibility with different environments. This will help identify
and fix potential issues before they impact users of your
library.

9. **Build Process**: Configure a build process that
compiles your TypeScript code into JavaScript, optimizes
the code for performance, and generates necessary type
definition files. Choose a module format (like UMD or
ESM) that is compatible with the target environment and
bundlers.

10. **Continuous Integration and Deployment**: Set up
continuous integration and deployment (CI/CD) to automatically test, build, and publish new versions of your
library. This will help ensure the code remains stable and
new releases are available to users quickly.

6.7   Can you discuss potential issues with TypeScript's structural type system in large projects?

TypeScript's structural type system brings many benefits to JavaScript projects and can enhance the developer experience with type checking and better code understanding. However, there might be some potential downsides in large projects that are worth discussing. These issues include:

1. **Unintended type compatibility:**

In TypeScript, two types are considered compatible if they have the same structural shape. This can lead to unintuitive situations where TypeScript treats types as compatible even though they are conceptually different.

For example, consider the following two types:

```
type Person = {
  name: string;
  age: number;
};

type Car = {
  name: string;
  age: number;
};

let person: Person = { name: "Alice", age: 30 };
let car: Car = { name: "Tesla␣Model␣S", age: 3 };

car = person; // No error!
```

In this case, TypeScript allows the assignment 'car = person' because both types have the same properties, even though they represent entirely different concepts. Resolving this issue might require adding additional properties to differentiate the types, using opaque types or unique symbols, or leveraging more refined type-checking options.

2. **Difficulty in refactoring:**

In large projects, structural typing can make refactoring more challenging. Changing a type's structure could affect many other types that are implicitly compatible due to their structural properties.

3. **Excess property checks for object literals:**

TypeScript only performs an excess property check when assigning an object literal directly to a type with an index signature or reading from the index signature. This can lead to errors in large projects where developers might define and pass objects with more properties than expected.

For example:

```
type Data = {
  prop1: string;
};

function processData(data: Data): void {
  console.log(data);
}

const obj = {
  prop1: "value",
  prop2: 42,
};

// No excess property check
processData(obj);

// Excess property check
```

```
processData({
  prop1: "value",
  prop2: 42, // Error: Object literal may only specify known
      properties
});
```

For large projects with many functions and object types,
constant object literal usage may cause performance issues
from excess property checks or unintended type errors.

4. **Verbose type annotations:**

TypeScript's structural types can sometimes result in verbose or complex type annotations, particularly for functions that work with generic types. In large projects, this
might cause readability issues and negatively impact the
maintainability of the code.

5. **Limited nominal typing support:**

While TypeScript primarily focuses on structural typing,
nominal typing support is limited, making it difficult to
establish relationships between types explicitly.

You can use some workarounds to mimic nominal typing
like "branded types" or "tagged types." However, these
solutions might feel more like hacks compared to a built-
in nominal typing mechanism.

For example, Branded types:

```
type PersonID = number & {readonly __brand: unique symbol};
type CarID = number & {readonly __brand: unique symbol};

function getPerson(id: PersonID) { /* ... */ }
function getCar(id: CarID) { /* ... */ }
```

```
const personId: PersonID = 42 as PersonID;
const carId: CarID = 42 as CarID;

getPerson(personId);
getCar(carId);
```

To summarize, TypeScript's structural type system generally brings many advantages to large projects, but there
are potential concerns to be cautious about. With careful design, clear guidelines, and thorough understanding,
developers can make better decisions in leveraging Type-
Script's typing features within their projects.

6.8   Can you discuss the impact of enabling "strict" mode in TypeScript on a large scale project?

Enabling "strict" mode in TypeScript can have significant
impact on a large scale project. "strict" mode is a compiler option that enforces stricter type checking and improves code maintainability in TypeScript. In this mode,
TypeScript detects several common errors early and ensures type safety. To enable "strict" mode, add the following line to the 'tsconfig.json' file:

```
{
  "compilerOptions": {
    "strict": true
  }
}
```

There are several advantages and challenges when using
"strict" mode in TypeScript, especially for a large scale
project. Let's discuss some key points:

1. **Type Safety**: The primary objective of "strict"
mode is to enforce type safety. This means that Type-
Script will ensure that all values assigned to a variable,
function, or property conform to the expected type. For
example:

```
function add(a: number, b: number): number {
  return a + b;
}
```

In this example, the 'add' function expects two parameters (a and b) of type 'number' and returns a 'number'.
In "strict" mode, assigning an incorrect type value will
result in a compilation error.

2. **Increased Code Maintainability and Readability**:
"strict" mode forces developers to be more explicit regarding types and nullable values. This results in cleaner
code with well-defined types and makes it easier for other
developers to understand the codebase, improving maintainability and collaboration.

3. **Early Error Detection**: Catching errors at compile-
time instead of runtime can save valuable development
and debugging time. "strict" mode helps to detect several
common errors like:

- Undefined or null values

- Incompatible type assignments

- Missing return paths in a function

4. **Refactoring Safely**: The additional type information provided with "strict" mode helps developers refactor their code more safely. This is because any changes to types or values that could potentially break the code will be caught by the TypeScript compiler before runtime.

However, converting a large-scale project to "strict" mode is not without its challenges:

1. **Conversion Effort**: When enabling "strict" mode in an existing project, it is common to encounter numerous type-related issues. This requires developers to invest time and effort in fixing these issues or refactoring the code. While this can be time-consuming initially, it results in a more robust and maintainable codebase in the long run.

2. **Learning Curve**: For developers new to TypeScript, the additional type annotations and stricter type checking can be intimidating. However, with time and practice, developers become more familiar with the language and the benefits of type safety.

In conclusion, while enabling "strict" mode in TypeScript for a large scale project can be challenging initially, the benefits of enhanced code quality, improved maintainability, and reduced potential for errors make it a worthwhile investment.

As a final note, the following chart illustrates some aspects of "strict" mode:

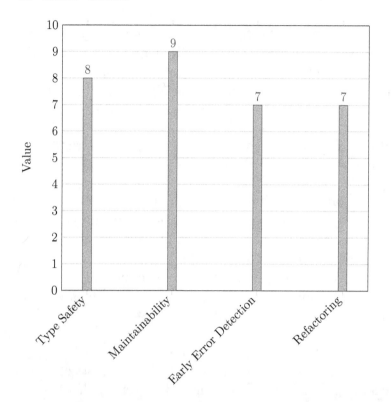

Here, the positive values indicate benefits of using "strict"
mode, while negative values represent challenges faced
when enabling "strict" mode in a large scale project.

6.9 How would you tackle performance optimization for TypeScript transpilation in a large, complex codebase?

Optimizing the TypeScript transpilation process in a large, complex codebase can be challenging, but there are several techniques and best practices to improve performance. Here, I'll walk you through some of the key approaches that you can adopt to get the most out of the TypeScript's transpilation:

1. **Incremental compilation and 'composite' projects**: Starting from TypeScript 3.0, you can use the '–incremental' flag or '"incremental": true' in your 'tsconfig.json' to enable incremental compilation. This allows TypeScript to build upon the previous compilation results, thus resulting in a faster build process.

In addition, if your codebase is organized into multiple interconnected modules or projects, consider using TypeScript's project references feature. By setting '"composite": true' in the 'tsconfig.json' file of each project/module, TypeScript will be able to efficiently build only the required projects, resulting in faster build times. This is particularly useful when working with monorepos or complex project structures.

Example 'tsconfig.json' with 'incremental' and 'composite' enabled:

```
{
  "compilerOptions": {
    "incremental": true,
    "composite": true,
    "target": "es6"
    // other compilerOptions...
  },
  "include": [
    "src/**/*.ts"
  ],
  "exclude": [
    "node_modules"
  ]
}
```

2. **Use 'skipLibCheck'**: By default, the TypeScript
compiler checks all '.d.ts' files in your codebase, which
can result in slower build times, especially when there
are numerous external dependencies. You can set the
'skipLibCheck' option in your 'tsconfig.json' to skip type-
checking these external declaration files, thus speeding up
the transpilation process.

```
{
  "compilerOptions": {
    "skipLibCheck": true
    // other compilerOptions...
  }
}
```

Note that using 'skipLibCheck' might result in some type
errors being left undetected. However, this risk might
be acceptable if the project relies on stable, widely-used
libraries.

3. **Type-checking and bundling in parallel**: When
building your TypeScript codebase, you can use tools like
'fork-ts-checker-webpack-plugin' in conjunction with 'web-

pack' to run type-checking and bundling processes concurrently. This can significantly speed up build times.

4. **Tweak transpilation options**: In some cases, changing compilation target or module type might result in faster build times or smaller output. For instance, you might consider targeting a more recent ECMAScript version, such as 'es2017', to take advantage of native support for features like async/await. The same holds for the 'module' option - e.g., if you're targeting browser environments, you might want to switch to 'esnext' modules.

5. **Optimize the codebase**: Keeping the codebase clean, modular, and optimized is a good practice for improving the overall performance of the transpilation process. Some ways to achieve this include:

- Remove unused imports and declarations.

- Use lazy-loading for heavy-weight modules.

- Typedef files (.d.ts) should be kept small, focusing on essential type information.

- Leverage TypeScript's '–noUnusedParameters' and '–noUnusedLocals' options (or an equivalent linting setup with ESLint) to catch and clean up unused code parts during development.

By employing these strategies to optimize the TypeScript transpilation in a large, complex codebase, you can ensure faster, more efficient build times and an improved development experience.

Keep in mind that performance optimization is an ongoing process, so it's essential to regularly monitor build times and look for new opportunities to make improvements. Good luck!

6.10 How do you enforce a consistent coding style and practices in a large TypeScript project?

Enforcing a consistent coding style and practices in a large TypeScript project can be achieved by using a combination of tools, guidelines, and processes. Some key aspects to consider include:

1. **Code Formatting**: To maintain a consistent code formatting, use tools like Prettier or TSLint. Prettier is an opinionated code formatter that supports TypeScript formatting. Install it as a dev dependency in your project and create a configuration file with your preferred settings (e.g. '.prettierrc'). Example configuration:

```
{
    "singleQuote": true,
    "trailingComma": "all",
    "tabWidth": 4,
    "printWidth": 80
}
```

2. **Linting**: Use TSLint or ESLint with TypeScript

plugin to enforce coding practices by defining linting rules. These rules help identify potential errors and enforce consistent style across the codebase.

3. **TypeScript Compiler Options**: Use the 'tsconfig.json' file to enforce strict typing and other coding practices. Some key options to consider include:

- '"noImplicitAny": true' to disallow implicit 'any' types.

- '"strictNullChecks": true' to ensure that null and undefined values are explicitly handled.

- '"noUnusedLocals": true' to report errors on unused local variables.

Full example config:

```
{
    "compilerOptions": {
        "target": "es2017",
        "module": "commonjs",
        "strict": true,
        "noImplicitAny": true,
        "strictNullChecks": true,
        "noUnusedLocals": true,
        "strictFunctionTypes": true,
        "strictPropertyInitialization": true,
        "sourceMap": true,
        "outDir": "./dist",
        "typeRoots": ["./node_modules/@types"],
        "lib": ["es2017", "dom"]
    },
    "include": ["src/**/*.ts"],
    "exclude": ["node_modules", "**/*.spec.ts", "dist"]
}
```

4. **Code Review**: Establish a code review process where every pull request is reviewed by at least one other team member. This process helps in maintaining code quality and ensuring adherence to the agreed-upon guide-

lines.

5. **Documentation**: Create a living style guide or a set of coding conventions for your project in a dedicated markdown file like 'CONTRIBUTING.md'. This document should outline the coding practices, patterns, and guidelines to be followed by all team members.

6. **Automate**: Implement Continuous Integration (CI) pipelines in your project. CI tools like GitHub Actions, GitLab CI, or Jenkins can automatically check code formatting, run linting, and build the project every time a new commit is pushed, ensuring that all changes comply with the established conventions.

In conclusion, enforcing a consistent coding style and practices in a large TypeScript project can be achieved by:

- Consistent code formatting with tools like Prettier

- Linting with TSLint or ESLint (with TypeScript plugin)

- Configuring 'tsconfig.json' with appropriate compiler options

- Regular code reviews

- Documentation of style guide and conventions

- Continuous Integration (CI) pipelines for automated checks

Following these practices will help ensure that your large TypeScript project maintains a consistent style and follows best practices, making it easier for your team to collaborate and maintain an easily understandable codebase.

6.11   How can TypeScript be leveraged to improve the design of Domain Driven Design (DDD) or Clean Architecture?

TypeScript can be leveraged to improve the design of Domain Driven Design (DDD) and Clean Architecture by providing a strong and statically typed language that ensures type safety, improved code maintainability, and better abstractions.

Here are some ways TypeScript improves the design of DDD or Clean Architecture projects:

1. **Using interfaces for designing Entities, Value Objects, and Aggregates:**

TypeScript provides the concept of interfaces, which allows defining a contract for custom types such as Entities, Value Objects, and Aggregates in a DDD project. These interfaces act as a blueprint for your domain, enabling better separation of concerns and enforcing structural rules in your codebase.

For example:

```
interface UserEntity {
  id: string;
  name: string;
  email: string;
}

class User implements UserEntity {
```

```
constructor(
  public id: string,
  public name: string,
  public email: string
) {}
}
```

2. **Implementing Repositories using Generics:**

TypeScript's support for generic types enables the creation of more reusable code, such as generic repositories in a DDD project. By leveraging TypeScript generics, you can create a single repository that works with any Entity, making it more efficient and easy to maintain.

For example, consider the following generic repository interface:

```
interface IRepository<T> {
  findById(id: string): Promise<T>;
  save(item: T): Promise<T>;
}
```

You can implement a specific User repository by extending the generic IRepository:

```
class UserRepository implements IRepository<User> {
  findById(id: string): Promise<User> {
    // ...
  }

  save(user: User): Promise<User> {
    // ...
  }
}
```

3. **Using TypeScript utility types for better abstractions:**

Utility types in TypeScript provide better flexibility and productivity while abstracting the codebase. You can use utility types like Partial, Readonly, Pick, and Exclude to create better encapsulated Value Objects and Entities, ensuring immutability and other design principles.

For example, using Readonly to make an Entity immutable:

```
type Immutable<T> = Readonly<T>;

class User {
  constructor(public readonly id: string, public data: Immutable<
      UserEntity>) {}
}
```

4. **Creating abstract classes for base Entities, Value Objects, and Aggregates:**

TypeScript provides support for abstract classes, which can act as a foundation for Entities, Value Objects, and Aggregates. These reusable components can encapsulate common logic and functionalities within your codebase, ensuring better DRY (Don't Repeat Yourself) principles and easier maintainability.

For example, here's an abstract base class for an Entity:

```
abstract class BaseEntity<T> {
  constructor(public id: string, public data: T) {}

  get(prop: keyof T): T[keyof T] {
    return this.data[prop];
  }
  set(prop: keyof T, value: T[keyof T]): void {
    this.data[prop] = value;
  }
}

class User extends BaseEntity<UserEntity> {}
```

5. **Type checking for invariant rules:**

By using TypeScript, you can build domain objects with type checking in place to ensure that your objects adhere to invariant rules. This makes refactoring and extending the domain model much more accessible while ensuring that errors are caught at compile-time rather than at runtime.

For example, creating a Domain Event with a required payload property:

```
interface DomainEvent<T> {
  type: string;
  payload: T;
}

function createDomainEvent<T>(type: string, payload: T):
    DomainEvent<T> {
  return { type, payload };
}

const userCreatedEvent = createDomainEvent("USER_CREATED", {
    userId: "1" });
```

In summary, TypeScript enhances DDD and Clean Architecture projects by providing static typing, interfaces, utility types, and other features that promote better abstractions, maintainability, and adherence to domain rules. With TypeScript, you can create a more expressive and robust domain model that adheres to DDD or Clean Architecture principles.

6.12   How do you manage the dependencies between different TypeScript projects in a monorepo?

When working with a monorepo in a TypeScript project, you need to manage the dependencies between different packages correctly. One way to do this efficiently is by using tools like Yarn workspaces, Lerna, or the native TypeScript 'Project References'.

Let's discuss each approach and how it can be used to manage dependencies in a monorepo.

1. Yarn Workspaces:

Yarn workspaces are a feature introduced in Yarn v1 to manage dependencies for monorepos. It allows you to have multiple packages within one repository and manage their dependencies efficiently, sharing common dependencies and avoiding duplicate installations.

To use Yarn workspaces, first, enable the feature in the 'package.json' at the root level:

```
{
  "name": "monorepo",
  "private": true,
  "workspaces": [
    "packages/*"
  ]
}
```

Here, the "packages/*" pattern means that all folders inside "packages" are considered workspaces for the monorepo.

Then, add a 'package.json' file in each package folder, specifying its dependencies. For common dependencies (e.g., TypeScript), specify them only in the root package.json to avoid duplicates.

2. Lerna:

Lerna is another tool for managing monorepos in JavaScript and TypeScript projects. It helps manage dependencies between packages, execute scripts across them, and publish packages to package registries like npm.

To use Lerna, first, install the Lerna CLI:

```
npm i -g lerna
```

Then, initialize Lerna in your monorepo:

```
lerna init
```

This command will create a 'lerna.json' configuration file and 'packages' folder for your monorepo.

Similar to Yarn workspaces, you should have a 'package.json' file in each package folder. You can use 'lerna bootstrap' to install dependencies for each package and symlink local packages in the monorepo.

3. TypeScript Project References:

TypeScript 3.0 introduced a new feature called "project references," which allows you to manage dependencies between TypeScript projects. This feature provides a way for TypeScript projects to depend on one another, improving build times and enforcing correct builds.

To use TypeScript project references, create a 'tsconfig.json' file for each package in your monorepo and set up the dependencies using the 'references' option.

For example, let's say you have two TypeScript packages, 'package-a' and 'package-b', where 'package-b' depends on 'package-a'. Your configuration files would look like this:

'package-a/tsconfig.json':

```
{
  "compilerOptions": {
    ...
  }
}
```

'package-b/tsconfig.json':

```
{
  "compilerOptions": {
    ...
  },
  "references": [
    { "path": "../package-a" }
  ]
}
```

Here, the reference in 'package-b/tsconfig.json' states that it depends on 'package-a'.

Now, to manage and build the entire monorepo, create a 'tsconfig.json' at the root level:

```
{
  "files": [],
  "references": [
    { "path": "./packages/package-a" },
    { "path": "./packages/package-b" }
  ]
}
```

Finally, use the 'tsc' command with the '–build' flag to build the entire monorepo, taking care of the dependencies:

```
tsc --build
```

Each approach has its benefits and use cases. Yarn workspaces and Lerna handle more than just TypeScript-specific configurations and have advanced features for dependency management and publishing. TypeScript project references focus on build dependencies and improving build times. In many cases, combining these approaches (e.g., using Yarn Workspaces or Lerna alongside TypeScript project references) results in an efficient setup for managing TypeScript monorepos.

6.13 How can you leverage TypeScript's type system for better error handling and failure recovery at runtime?

Typescript's type system strongly focuses on providing static type checking and catching errors during development to ensure code correctness before runtime. While it doesn't directly offer runtime error handling and recovery mechanisms, there are still various ways you can leverage Typescript features to write better error handling and recovery solutions.

1. Advanced types for function inputs and outputs:

You can create more specific types to enforce your functions' inputs and outputs, which can lead to better self-documenting code and make error handling more straightforward.

For example, imagine you have a function that takes an input and returns a 'Result' type that contains an error message, if any:

```
type Result<T> = { success: true; data: T } | { success: false;
    error: string };

function myFunction(input: number): Result<number> {
  if (input < 0) {
    return { success: false, error: "Negative number not allowed"
        };
  }

  // Do some processing
```

```
  const result = input * 2;

  return { success: true, data: result };
}
const result = myFunction(-5);
if (!result.success) {
  console.error(result.error);
} else {
  console.log(result.data);
}
```

By using the 'Result' type, you express the possible failure explicitly and force yourself and other developers to handle it during runtime.

2. Custom error classes:

You can create custom error classes that provide additional context about the error and make it easier to handle particular error scenarios:

```
class MyError extends Error {
  constructor(public code: number, message?: string) {
    super(message);
  }
}
```

Then in your functions, you can throw or catch these custom errors and handle them according to the error codes:

```
function throwError(): never {
  throw new MyError(404, "Not found");
}

try {
  throwError();
} catch (error) {
  if (error instanceof MyError) {
    console.error(`Error with code ${error.code}: ${error.message
        }`);
  } else {
    console.error(`Unknown error: ${error.message}`);
```

```
    }
  }
```

3. Type guards and discriminated unions:

If you're dealing with different kinds of errors and their
handling, you can write discriminated unions for these
errors and use type guards to enforce a specific handling
process based on their type.

```
type APIError = { type: "APIError"; statusCode: number; message:
    string };
type ValidationError = { type: "ValidationError"; errors: string[]
    };

type AppError = APIError | ValidationError;

function handleAppError(error: AppError) {
  if (isAPIError(error)) {
    // Handle APIError
    console.error(`API Error: Status - ${error.statusCode}, Message
      - ${error.message}`);
  } else {
    // Handle ValidationError
    console.error(`Validation Errors: ${error.errors.join(", ")}`);
  }
}

function isAPIError(error: AppError): error is APIError {
  return error.type === "APIError";
}

const apiError: APIError = {
  type: "APIError",
  statusCode: 404,
  message: "Not Found",
};

const validationError: ValidationError = {
  type: "ValidationError",
  errors: ["Name is required", "Email is invalid"],
};

handleAppError(apiError);
handleAppError(validationError);
```

Here, the 'AppError' type is a union of 'APIError' and

'ValidationError'. The custom type guard 'isAPIError'
helps in identifying the error type and handling it accordingly.

While TypeScript can't catch all runtime errors, the features mentioned above can help you build better error
handling mechanisms in your TypeScript projects. Although TypeScript doesn't modify the runtime behavior
of JavaScript, these techniques ensure that you and your
teammates consider error cases resulting in more robust
code.

6.14   Can you describe how to cre-
ate custom type guards for
complex types in TypeScript?

Custom type guards are functions that make it easier for
TypeScript to identify the proper type of a variable during
runtime. They can be especially useful when dealing with
complex types made up of multiple interfaces or types,
such as discriminated unions or intersection types.

Let's go through the process of creating custom type guards
step by step with an example.

Suppose we have a complex type that can be either a
'Circle' or a 'Rectangle', represented by the following interfaces:

```
interface Circle {
  kind: 'circle';
  radius: number;
}

interface Rectangle {
  kind: 'rectangle';
  width: number;
  height: number;
}
```

To define a custom type guard, you need a function that takes a parameter of a more general type (e.g., 'unknown' or 'any') and returns a boolean, with a 'type predicate' as the return type. Here's an example of a type guard for the 'Circle' type:

```
function isCircle(shape: unknown): shape is Circle {
  return (shape as Circle).kind === 'circle';
}
```

In the example above, we're taking an 'unknown' parameter 'shape' and use a type assertion to check whether its 'kind' property is equal to 'circle'. If this condition is true, TypeScript can infer that the 'shape' parameter is of type 'Circle'.

Following the same pattern, you can create a type guard for the 'Rectangle' type:

```
function isRectangle(shape: unknown): shape is Rectangle {
  return (shape as Rectangle).kind === 'rectangle';
}
```

Now, let's use our custom type guards with a function that calculates the area of a given shape:

```
type Shape = Circle | Rectangle;
```

```
function area(shape: Shape): number {
  if (isCircle(shape)) {
    return Math.PI * shape.radius * shape.radius;
  } else if (isRectangle(shape)) {
    return shape.width * shape.height;
  } else {
    throw new Error('Invalid␣shape␣type');
  }
}
```

In the 'area' function, we make use of our custom type guards 'isCircle' and 'isRectangle' to check whether the input shape is a 'Circle' or a 'Rectangle'. Once the type guard is confirmed by TypeScript, we have access to the specific properties of that type, like 'radius', 'width', and 'height'.

To summarize, custom type guards can be created by defining a function that takes a parameter of a general type and returns a boolean with a type predicate. These type guards greatly enhance TypeScript's ability to infer types during runtime, particularly for complex types made up of multiple interfaces or other types.

6.15   What strategies would you employ to gradually adopt Type-Script in a large JavaScript project?

Gradually adopting TypeScript in a large JavaScript project can be a challenging task, as it normally involves proper planning, refactoring, and training for the development team. While TypeScript offers a lot of benefits, such as better type safety, improved IntelliSense, and a more robust development experience, it is important to ensure a smooth and efficient transition from JavaScript.

Here are some strategies to consider when gradually adopting TypeScript in a large JavaScript project:

1. **Evaluate the project and set realistic goals**: Perform an initial assessment of the JavaScript project to identify the most critical areas that could benefit from TypeScript. Do a cost-benefit analysis considering factors like the size of the project, available resources, and time constraints. Set realistic goals to address project requirements.

2. **Integrate TypeScript gradually into the existing build process**: As you start the conversion, configure your build system to allow both JavaScript and TypeScript files. Use well-defined steps and automation tools like Webpack, Babel, or TSC (TypeScript compiler) to make sure the build process doesn't break.

3. **Incremental typing**: TypeScript supports a gradual typing system, which allows you to gradually add type annotations to your JavaScript code. This means, you can start the conversion by renaming your JavaScript files from *.js to *.ts, and then gradually add type definitions without having to refactor the entire codebase at once.

4. **Start with the most critical components**: Focus

on adding TypeScript to the most critical areas or components of the project that have a higher likelihood of introducing bugs or require frequent changes. This would help to minimize errors and enhance code maintainability in the long run.

5. **Add strict type-checking gradually**: TypeScript offers various strictness options that you can enable or disable according to your needs. You can start with less strict settings and gradually increase strictness as your team gets more familiar with TypeScript.

6. **Use TypeScript with existing libraries**: Consider utilizing TypeScript type definitions for popular JavaScript libraries to ensure proper type checking and IntelliSense when using library functions. You can find type definitions in the DefinitelyTyped repository or in the library's official documentation.

7. **Continuously refactor the codebase**: As you add TypeScript to your project, continue refactoring the codebase to leverage TypeScript features such as interfaces, classes, and modules. This will enhance code maintainability, readability, and testability.

8. **Train the development team**: Educate your development team about TypeScript, its benefits, and best practices. Encourage the team to follow a consistent coding style and promote peer code reviews to ensure the quality of the codebase.

Here's a chart visualizing the gradual adoption of Type-

Script in a project:

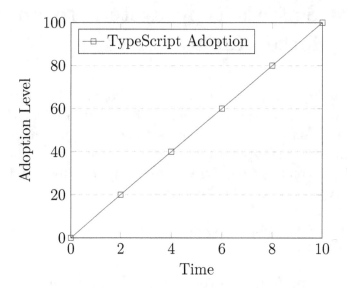

As you gradually adopt TypeScript in your project, remember that it is a continuous process that requires constant review and updating of design patterns, code quality, and team knowledge. By following these strategies,
you can ensure a smooth transition to TypeScript and
gain the full benefits it offers.

6.16   How would you use Type-Script's type system to enforce immutability?

Immutability is a powerful concept in programming that helps prevent unintended side effects in a codebase by ensuring that once a variable or object is created, it cannot be modified. In TypeScript, we can enforce immutability using a combination of 'readonly', mapped types, and utility types such as 'ReadonlyArray'.

Let's see some examples of how we can achieve immutability in TypeScript:

1. **Using 'readonly'**: You can use the 'readonly' keyword with properties to enforce that they cannot be modified after being initialized.

```
class ImmutablePoint {
  readonly x: number;
  readonly y: number;

  constructor(x: number, y: number) {
    this.x = x;
    this.y = y;
  }
}

const point = new ImmutablePoint(3, 4);
point.x = 5; // Error: Cannot assign to 'x' because it is a read-
    only property
```

2. **Using mapped types**: Mapped types allow you to create a new type based on an existing type, with some transformations applied to its properties. To make all properties of a type read-only, we can use a mapped type:

```
type Readonly<T> = {
  readonly [P in keyof T]: T[P];
};

interface Point {
  x: number;
  y: number;
}

const mutablePoint: Point = { x: 3, y: 4 };
mutablePoint.x = 5; // OK

const immutablePoint: Readonly<Point> = { x: 3, y: 4 };
immutablePoint.x = 5; // Error: Cannot assign to 'x' because it is
    a read-only property
```

Here, 'Readonly<T>' is a mapped type that enforces all
properties of 'T' to be read-only using 'readonly'.

3. **Using utility types**: TypeScript provides some
built-in utility types such as 'ReadonlyArray' and 'Read-
only<T>' that can help enforce immutability:

- 'ReadonlyArray<T>': Enforces immutability for arrays.

```
const mutableArray: number[] = [1, 2, 3];
mutableArray.push(4); // OK

const immutableArray: ReadonlyArray<number> = [1, 2, 3];
immutableArray.push(4); // Error: Property 'push' does not exist on
    type 'ReadonlyArray<number>'
```

- 'Readonly<T>': This utility type is essentially the same
as the mapped type we defined in the previous step.

```
const immutablePoint: Readonly<Point> = { x: 3, y: 4 };
immutablePoint.x = 5; // Error: Cannot assign to 'x' because it is
    a read-only property
```

In summary, TypeScript's type system allows us to enforce immutability by using the 'readonly' keyword, creating mapped types, and leveraging built-in utility types

like 'ReadonlyArray' and 'Readonly<T>'. These tools
applied together help to ensure that developers adhere to
the principles of immutability, leading to safer and more
maintainable code.

6.17   What are the best practices to handle 'any' types in a large TypeScript project?

Handling 'any' types in a large TypeScript project can be
tricky, but the following best practices help maintain a
strict, type-safe environment that leads to fewer bugs and
improved maintainability.

1. **Minimize usage of 'any'**: Avoid using the 'any'
type as much as possible. It disables type checking and
could cause unexpected runtime issues. Instead, opt for
strict types or use union types where necessary.

2. **Use 'unknown' when applicable**: If you have a
value that could be of any type and you want to enforce a
type check before using it, use the 'unknown' type instead
of 'any'. An 'unknown' type forces developers to perform
type checking or type narrowing before using the value.

Example:

```
function handleValue(value: unknown): number {
  if (typeof value === "number") {
    return value;
```

```
  } else {
    throw new Error("Value must be a number.");
  }
}
```

3. **Type assertions**: If you are certain about a value's type, you can use type assertions to convert between types. This should only be used with caution after proper checks are in place.

Example:

```
function handleValue(value: unknown): number {
  if (typeof value === "number") {
    return value as number;
  } else {
    throw new Error("Value must be a number.");
  }
}
```

4. **Leverage 'type guards'**: Use custom type guard functions to safely handle different types.

Example:

```
type Animal = { type: "dog"; age: number } | { type: "cat"; age:
    number };

function isDog(animal: Animal): animal is { type: "dog"; age:
    number } {
  return animal.type === "dog";
}

function handleAnimal(animal: Animal) {
  if (isDog(animal)) {
    console.log("Handling a dog of age", animal.age);
  } else {
    console.log("Handling a cat of age", animal.age);
  }
}
```

5. **Use third-party type-safe libraries**: When using

third-party libraries that don't have type definitions, prefer using libraries that have type-safe alternatives. For
example, for Lodash, use 'lodash-ts' or consult 'DefinitelyTyped' for type definitions.

6. **Employ strict mode**: In your 'tsconfig.json' file,
enable the 'strict' flag or enable 'strictNullChecks', 'strict-
FunctionTypes', and other related flags individually. This
will make TypeScript more strict and require your code
to be more type-safe.

Example 'tsconfig.json':

```
{
  "compilerOptions": {
    "strict": true,
    /* or enable individual flags */
    "strictNullChecks": true,
    "strictFunctionTypes": true
  }
}
```

In summary, try to minimize the use of 'any' types in your
TypeScript projects. Use 'unknown' when applicable, apply type assertions responsibly, leverage type guards, prefer type-safe third-party libraries, and enable strict mode
to help maintain a type-safe and more maintainable code
base.

6.18   Can you discuss some strategies for debugging complex type errors in TypeScript?

Debugging complex type errors in TypeScript can be a challenging task. Here, I will outline some strategies to tackle this task more effectively. These strategies range from using type annotations and narrowing, to leveraging utility types and improving error messages.

1. **Divide and Conquer**

Break down the faulty code into smaller parts, and check types at each step. This will often help you narrow down the problematic part of the code. You can use explicit type annotations to ensure you're using the correct type at various points in your code.

For example, let's say you have a complex function manipulating arrays and objects:

```
function complexFunction(data: SomeType[]): ReturnType {
  // complex array manipulation
  // complex object manipulation

  return finalData;
}
```

Add type annotations at specific stages to check if the types align with what you expect:

```
function complexFunction(data: SomeType[]): ReturnType {
  const arrayResult: IntermediateArrayType = ... // complex array
    manipulation
```

```
const objectResult: IntermediateObjectType = ... // complex
    object manipulation
return finalData;
}
```

2. **Type Lemmas**

When debugging recursive types or higher-order types, it can be helpful to define simplified types that are equivalent (in terms of their behavior) to the original type. These simplified types are often easier to understand in terms of error messages when things go wrong.

Consider the following recursive type representing a nested array:

```
type RecursiveArray<T> = T[] | RecursiveArray<T>[];
```

If the error messages involving 'RecursiveArray' become complex, try creating a simplified, analogous type for debugging purposes:

```
type SimpleRecursiveArray<T> = T[] | (T | SimpleRecursiveArray<T>)
    [];
// then use SimpleRecursiveArray instead of RecursiveArray for
    debugging purposes
```

3. **Type Narrowing**

Using TypeScript's built-in type narrowing techniques, such as 'typeof', 'instanceof', user-defined type guards, or the 'in' operator, can help eliminate potential type mismatches and make it easier to track down type-related bugs.

```
function isString(val: unknown): val is string {
  return typeof val === 'string';
}

function doSomething(input: string | number | undefined) {
  if (isString(input)) {
    // TypeScript now knows input is a string.
  } else if (typeof input === 'number') {
    // TypeScript now knows input is a number.
  } else {
    // input must be undefined.
  }
}
```

4. **Leveraging Utility types**

TypeScript provides a variety of [utility types](https://www
.typescriptlang.org/docs/handbook/utility-types.html) that
make it easy to perform type manipulation. When working with complex types, these utility types can help simplify and clarify your types.

Use utility types such as 'Partial<T>', 'Required<T>',
'Readonly<T>', 'Record<K,T>', 'Pick<T,K>', and
'Omit<T,K>' to transform the type and receive better
insight and control over the types you are working with.

5. **Improve error messages**

TypeScript 4.1 introduced [Template Literal Types](https://
www.typescriptlang.org/docs/handbook/2/template-literal-
types.html) which can help you in generating human-
readable error messages using type-level programming.

```
type ErrorIfNotString<T> = T extends string ? T : `Type '${T}' is
    not a string`;

// The following will produce an error: Type 'number' is not a
    string
type Test = ErrorIfNotString<number>;
```

6. **Reading Compiler Error Messages**

TypeScript error messages typically show the "source" type and the "target" type that are not compatible with each other. Make sure you understand the structure of the TypeScript errors: 'TS<number>' refers to error number, followed by the error message in detail. Read these messages and understand how they provide meaningful insights into type errors.

7. **Visual Debugging**

Sometimes, visualizing your types could make it easy to understand complex type errors. Plotting the shape of the type or creating UML-like class diagrams may clarify the error. For example, you can visualize nested types as trees.

8. **Using Visual Studio Code or any compatible IDE**

Visual Studio Code, and other TypeScript-aware IDEs, can give you crucial real-time feedback on your types and help you navigate type errors effectively. With the context-aware autocompletion, suggestions, and inline error reporting, these IDEs can significantly improve your troubleshooting process.

In conclusion, debugging complex type errors in Type-Script calls for a combination of strategies. These include breaking down code, defining intermediate types, using type narrowing techniques, leveraging utility types, improving error messages, understanding TypeScript errors,

visualizing types, and utilizing powerful IDEs like Visual
Studio Code.

6.19 How would you approach implementing multi-threading in a TypeScript project?

To implement multi-threading in a TypeScript project,
your best option is to use Web Workers. Web Workers are
a web technology that allows you to run JavaScript code
in the background, effectively enabling multi-threading
capabilities. They run in a separate, isolated environment and communicate with the main thread using the
postMessage method and event listeners.

Here's a high-level approach to implementing multi-threading
in a TypeScript project using Web Workers:

1. Create the worker file:

Create a separate TypeScript file for your worker, let's
call it "worker.ts". This file will contain the code to be
executed in the background.

>Add your worker logic

worker.ts:

```
self.onmessage = (event: MessageEvent) => {
  const data = event.data;
```

```
// Process the data, perform calculations
const result = doSomeHeavyProcessing(data);

// Send the result back to the main thread
(self as any).postMessage(result);
};

function doSomeHeavyProcessing(data: any): any {
// Perform your heavy calculations here
// ...
return result;
}
```

2. Create the main file

Create the main TypeScript file, let's call it "main.ts".
This file will create the Web Worker, send data to the
worker, and listen for results.

main.ts:

```
// Create a worker from the worker.ts file
const worker = new Worker(new URL("./worker.ts", import.meta.url))
    ;

// Send data to the worker
worker.postMessage({...someData});

// Listen for results from the worker
worker.onmessage = (event: MessageEvent) => {
  console.log("Result received from worker:", event.data);
};
```

3. Compilation: Since the Worker constructor expects
a URL as its argument, you'll need to properly configure your build process (e.g., using Webpack or Rollup) to
bundle your worker code and obtain a URL for it.

Using Webpack, you should configure 'worker-loader' in
your Webpack configuration:

webpack.config.js:

```
module.exports = {
  // Your normal Webpack configuration
  module: {
    rules: [
      // Specific rule for workers
      {
        test: /.worker.ts$/,
        loader: "worker-loader",
        options: {
          inline: "fallback",
          filename: "workers/[contenthash].js",
        },
      },
      // Other rules
    ],
  },
};
```

4. Using Promises and async/await:

You can also leverage Promises and the async/await syntax to make your multi-threading implementation cleaner and more in line with modern JavaScript practices.

main.ts (using async/await):

```
async function getResultFromWorker(data: any): Promise<any> {
  return new Promise((resolve) => {
    // Create the worker
    const worker = new Worker(new URL("./worker.ts", import.meta.
        url));

    // Send the data to the worker
    worker.postMessage(data);

    // Listen for results from the worker
    worker.onmessage = (event: MessageEvent) => {
      worker.terminate(); // Terminate the worker after receiving
          the result
      resolve(event.data); // Resolve the Promise with the result
    };
  });
}

(async () => {
```

```
const result = await getResultFromWorker({...someData});
console.log("Result received from worker:", result);
})();
```

In summary, to implement multi-threading in a Type-
Script project, you should use Web Workers as they provide a strong foundation for running tasks concurrently.
Make sure to properly configure your build system to handle worker files, and consider using Promises and async/await
for a more modern implementation.

6.20   How can TypeScript be used effectively with data science or machine learning libraries?

TypeScript can be used effectively with data science and
machine learning libraries by providing a strong typing
system, better tooling support, higher code quality, and
seamless integration with popular libraries.

In the context of data science and machine learning, Type-
Script has several benefits. It is a superset of JavaScript,
which means you have access to the vast ecosystem of
JavaScript libraries for data processing, visualization, and
machine learning. At the same time, TypeScript's static
typing helps you catch errors early, which is important
when working with complex data structures and algorithms.

Here are some approaches and tips on how to effectively use TypeScript in combination with data science or machine learning libraries:

1. Select and use TypeScript-compatible libraries:

Several popular JavaScript libraries have TypeScript typings available, either included in the package or as separate '@types' packages. This allows you to work with these libraries seamlessly in TypeScript. Some examples are:

- TensorFlow.js: A machine learning library that runs in the browser or Node.js environment. It also provides TypeScript support out-of-the-box, so you can import and use it directly in your TypeScript projects.

- Danfo.js: A library for data manipulation and analysis, inspired by Python's Pandas library. It is written in TypeScript and provides comprehensive type definitions.

- D3.js: A visualization library that can be easily used with TypeScript by installing the '@types/d3' package.

2. Create TypeScript interfaces for data structures:

When dealing with data, it is essential to have a clear understanding of the data structures you are working with. In TypeScript, you can create interfaces to represent your data structures, making your code easier to understand and maintain. For example, if you have a dataset of students, you can define an interface like this:

```
interface Student {
  id: number;
  name: string;
  age: number;
  score: number;
}
```

3. Use type guards and type assertions:

In some cases, you may need to perform runtime checks to ensure that the data you're working with matches the expected shape. TypeScript's type guards and type assertions can help here. For example, a custom type guard can be used to filter out invalid data:

```
function isValidStudent(student: any): student is Student {
  return typeof student.id === 'number'
    && typeof student.name === 'string'
    && typeof student.age === 'number'
    && typeof student.score === 'number';
}

const validStudents = data.filter(isValidStudent);
```

4. Leverage TypeScript's advanced type system:

TypeScript offers various advanced type features such as generics, conditional types, and mapped types. These can be beneficial when working with complex data structures and algorithms in data science and machine learning. For instance, a generic function to handle data processing tasks can be written as:

```
function processData<T>(input: T[], processingFn: (data: T) => T):
    T[] {
  return input.map(processingFn);
}
```

5. Utilize external type declarations:

In case you're working with a library that doesn't have built-in TypeScript support nor separate '@types' package available, you can create your own type declaration files ('.d.ts') for these libraries. These declarations help TypeScript understand the structure and expected types from such libraries.

6. Use Promises and async/await:

Data processing and machine learning operations can often be time-consuming. Using Promises and the async/await syntax in TypeScript can help you manage asynchronous operations and improve code readability.

```
async function trainModel(dataset: TrainingData): Promise<Model> {
  /* ... */
}

const model = await trainModel(trainingData);
```

In summary, TypeScript can be effectively used with data science and machine learning libraries by leveraging its strong typing system, advanced type features, and seamless integration with supported libraries. By following these approaches, you can improve the reliability and maintainability of your data science and machine learning projects.